SEVEN LETTERS

Kathi Pelton

Hillsboro, OR

Copyright ©2024 Kathi Pelton

All rights reserved. No part of this publication may be reproduced, stored in a retrieval system, or transmitted in any form or by any means—for example, electronic, photocopy, recording—without the prior written permission of the publisher. The only exception is brief quotations in critical reviews.

Published by Inscribe Press, Hillsboro, OR.
Cover by Pelton Media Group, Locust Grove, VA.

Printed in the United States of America.

ISBN 978-1-951611-61-3

Unless otherwise indicated, all Scripture quotations are taken from the Holy Bible, New Living Translation, copyright © 1996, 2004, 2015 by Tyndale House Foundation. Used by permission of Tyndale House Publishers, Carol Stream, Illinois 60188. All rights reserved.

Scripture quotations marked (NIV) are taken from the Holy Bible, New International Version®, NIV®. Copyright © 1973, 1978, 1984, 2011 by Biblica, Inc.™ Used by permission of Zondervan. All rights reserved worldwide. www.zondervan.com The "NIV" and "New International Version" are trademarks registered in the United States Patent and Trademark Office by Biblica, Inc.™

Scripture quotations marked (AMPCE) are taken from the Amplified Bible, Copyright © 1954, 1958, 1962, 1964, 1965, 1987 by The Lockman Foundation. Used by permission.

Contents

Foreword ix
Introduction 1
Letter I 7
Letter II 19
Letter III 29
Letter IV 43
Letter V 61
Letter VI 81
Letter VII 99
Afterword 113
Sources 117
About the Author 119

Foreword

Occasionally there is a book which is not just a good book expounding biblical truth, but which is a book expressing truth essential for that season; truth that is being spotlighted by the Lord for a specific generation. *Seven Letters* is a book that should be essential reading for equipping those living in this season of the end-time birth pangs.

Kathi Pelton is a true daughter of the "tribe of Issachar"—those who understand the times and the seasons and know what the people of God need to do to be prepared for the times into which they were born.

The Book of Revelation is first and foremost the revelation of Jesus Christ. In these times, we need to know the Jesus revealed in the Book of Revelation and not just the Jesus revealed in the Gospels. As Kathy mines deeply the messages to the seven churches in the Book of Revelation, she keeps Jesus central. She shines light on him as the only One full of both grace and truth. She shines light on him as fully holy and fully merciful.

And Kathi does this in a way that makes the messages to the seven church of the Book of Revelation understandable and relevant for the times in which we live. She brings both challenge and encouragement as she shares so vulnerably and openly from her own life experiences.

This is clearly not a book written just to write another book. It is a book written under the inspiration of the Holy Spirit to help each one of us, as he repeats to each of the seven churches of Revelation to "hear what the Spirit is saying to the churches."

Rick Ridings, Founder/Director

Succat Hallel 24/7 House of Prayer and Worship

(overlooking the Temple Mount in Jerusalem)

Author and Elder in the Global Prayer movement

Introduction

Nestled in the opening pages of the book of Revelation are seven very personal and passionate letters from Jesus to his followers in seven cities around the Roman province of Asia. The Lord appeared to the Apostle John and gave him messages for the seven churches in those cities: Ephesus, Smyrna, Pergamum, Thyatira, Sardis, Philadelphia, and Laodicea. John faithfully recorded the words of Jesus and sent them to the churches to usher them into refinement, redemption, and the restoration of God's original intent and design for them. The Lord's words overflowed with exhortation, counsel, and correction—a mighty river of discipline, mercy, and grace drenching them in the greatness of his wisdom and love.

As a loving father brings counsel and correction to his children that he loves, the Lord was reminding his early church who they were and was bringing correction to the areas in which they had fallen away from his plans and purposes—and his perfect love. He was calling them back into the fullness of his love and ways.

As I read these letters in our present day, there has been a deep stirring building in my spirit, "Take heed! The

VII LETTERS

Counsel of the Almighty is speaking to his church today from these poignant letters." His mercy is once again being poured out like water to wash us, like fire to refine us, and like oil to keep our lampstands burning bright.

Will we take to heart the counsel of the Lord, spoken thousands of years ago? If we will, I believe that we will see a Third Great Awakening and a *revival of holiness* come upon the earth. God has come to revive and resuscitate his church by blowing his breath on our smoldering wick to once again be a light to the nations. This will not only cause his church to repent of compromise and embrace the holiness of the Lord, but it will also display genuine oneness with God and his Bride that will cause the world to know that Jesus is Messiah.

> *"My prayer is not for them alone. I pray also for those who will believe in me through their message, that all of them may be one, Father, just as you are in me, and I am in you. May they also be in us so that the world may believe that you have sent me. I have given them the glory that you gave me, that they may be one as we are one—I in them and you in me—so that they may be brought to complete unity. Then the world will know that you sent me and have loved them even as you have loved me." [John 17:20-23]*

This is the last recorded prayer of Jesus before he went to the cross. Heeding his counsel leads us into the unity that he planned and has greatly desired. But the fruit of compromise is a harvest of petty divisions and dishonor that keep us from oneness with God and oneness from

introduction

each other. As we rid ourselves of compromise and embrace humility, we come into the glory of his love, and then *"The world will know."* These verses have been my life prayer, and everything I do is based on the hope and belief that we can fulfill the prayer our Savior poured out in his last day on earth.

Each of the seven letters to the churches holds keys that we can implement as we ask the Spirit of God to revive our hearts and lives. It is easy to look at the warnings and corrections in the letters and thank God that we are not like the people he addressed; yet, are we truly different? Are there things that the Lord has against us that we need to heed?

> *The seven letters precede the prophecies because the Church must be zealous and holy to face the spiritual warfare of the Last Days...these letters are a preparation for God's People. Even though these letters were addressed to these specific first-century churches, they all have tremendous implications for God's People in the Last Days.*[1]

I have seen a great repentance and refinement happening in God's remnant people, but I sense that there are still so many who have become lukewarm or disheartened; and a multitude who have yet to come to know Christ. The heavenly Father is not satisfied with a few; he desires that all will inherit eternal life through his Son Jesus. He aches to see that none perish but all come to repentance.

---

1 Daniel C. Juster, ThD, *Passover: The Key that Unlocks the Book of Revelation* (Clarksville, MD: Lederer Books, 2011), 14.

VII LETTERS

Beloved, do not let this one thing escape your notice: With the Lord a day is like a thousand years, and a thousand years are like a day. The Lord is not slow in keeping his promise, as some understand slowness. Instead, he is patient with you, not wanting anyone to perish, but everyone to come to repentance.
[1 Peter 3:8-9]

I truly believe that the letters in Revelation are words of life to his end-time Bride. As we continue to revisit them, we can ask the Spirit of God to move in power and life, restoring and redeeming us and granting us the fear of the Lord. The counsel in these letters will create a pathway to the oneness with Jesus that he prayed for in John 17. His counsel springs from his love, patience, and covenant that was established thousands of years ago with Abraham. I also believe this is the bridge that will, one day soon, open the eyes of the Jewish people to see that their long-awaited Messiah was revealed two thousand years ago. (There is a discussion of this on pages 88-90.)

As we journey through this book, we will examine each letter and have opportunity to ask the Spirit of the Lord to refine us, purify us, and give us eyes to see and ears to hear what the Spirit is saying to the church of today.

introduction

"As for the mystery of the seven stars that you saw in my right hand, and the seven golden lampstands, the seven stars are the angels of the seven churches, and the seven lampstands are the seven churches."

Revelation 1:20

LETTER ONE

Ephesus

"To the angel of the church in Ephesus write: 'These are the words of him who holds the seven stars in his right hand and walks among the seven golden lampstands. I know your deeds, your hard work and your perseverance. I know that you cannot tolerate wicked people, that you have tested those who claim to be apostles but are not and have found them false. You have persevered and have endured hardships for my name and have not grown weary.
Yet I hold this against you: You have forsaken the love you had at first. Consider how far you have fallen! Repent and do the things you did at first. If you do not repent, I will come to you and remove your lampstand from its place. But you have this in your favor: You hate the practices of the Nicolaitans, which I also hate. Whoever has ears, let them hear what the Spirit says to the churches. To the one who is victorious, I will give the right to eat from the tree of life, which is in the paradise of God.'" [Revelation 2:1-7]

The church in Ephesus was planted by the Apostle Paul. He made an initial visit while on his way to Antioch, then returned months later in AD 52. Ephesus was the Roman capital of the Asian province, with a population of about 200,000, and was one of the greatest cities in the Empire.[1]

---

1   Titus Kennedy, *The Essential Archaeological Guide to Bible Lands* (Eugene, OR: Harvest House, 2023), 309-310.

VII LETTERS

Acts 19 tells the story of Paul's return to Ephesus, where he laid his hands on twelve disciples who were then baptized in the Holy Spirit.

> *While Apollos was at Corinth, Paul took the road through the interior and arrived at Ephesus. There he found some disciples and asked them, "Did you receive the Holy Spirit when you believed?"*
> *They answered, "No, we have not even heard that there is a Holy Spirit."*
> *So Paul asked, "Then what baptism did you receive?"*
> *"John's baptism," they replied.*
> *Paul said, "John's baptism was a baptism of repentance. He told the people to believe in the one coming after him, that is, in Jesus." On hearing this, they were baptized in the name of the Lord Jesus. When Paul placed his hands on them, the Holy Spirit came on them, and they spoke in tongues and prophesied. There were about twelve men in all. [Acts 19:1-7]*

The formation of this church began with an introduction to the Holy Spirit through Paul, followed by the baptism of the Holy Spirit—where believers in Yeshua spoke in tongues and prophesied. These men experienced the baptism of repentance through John the Baptist, and then the baptism of power through the introduction to the Holy Spirit. For the church in Ephesus, repentance came first and then power followed. This is a pattern throughout the Scriptures that is important for us today. All too often, we see implementation of prophecy and power before the baptism of repentance. This can be a grievous mistake in evangelism. We must introduce new converts to repentance

> letter I [ephesus]

before encouraging them in the power gifts or the power will become polluted.

After Paul established the church, the Apostle John became the overseer who governed and watered the young planting. He dedicated a significant part of his life to it, so this letter must have held great sentimental value. The people began worshipping and serving in "first love" but eventually departed from it. More on that later.

This letter opens with describing the One speaking the words being inscribed by John. These are words from he who holds the seven stars in his right hand and walks among the seven golden lampstands. What does this mean and why is he describing himself in this way?.

The Lord is the One who not only created the stars in the universe, but he holds them in place. The stars shine with beauty and give light in the hours of darkness, and the ministers of his gospel are like earthly stars across the world, put in place to give light amid great darkness. Jesus holds the ministers of his gospel in his hands, and these letters are our assurance of his care so that we do not become falling stars that lose our light and die out. Intimate care is given to each of us who minister to the church and to the lost. The Lord is watching over his ministers who prepare his bride for his return.

It is Jesus's love for the global church that causes him to bring both exhortation and correction through this letter. The seven lampstands are the seven churches that he is addressing. Though he lives in heaven, he walks among the

VII LETTERS

churches on earth to intimately care for them and to examine them so that they do not lose their light.

John 15 describes our heavenly Father as the gardener. A good gardener will daily walk his garden to examine and care for each plant, to ensure that none of them will be lost to disease or harmful pests. Like a gardener, the Lord walks among the churches planted on the earth to water, fertilize, prune, and remove everything that might bring them harm. He looks for what is fruitful, and for what is damaged or missing.

> *"I am the true vine, and my Father is the gardener. He cuts off every branch in me that bears no fruit, while every branch that does bear fruit he prunes[a] so that it will be even more fruitful. You are already clean because of the word I have spoken to you. Remain in me, as I also remain in you. No branch can bear fruit by itself; it must remain in the vine. Neither can you bear fruit unless you remain in me. [John 15:1-4]*

In my early years as a believer, I did not understand the discipline that came from the heart of a loving father who was truly concerned for my heart and its condition. I was only familiar with a father who withdrew his attention when he didn't approve of my decisions or who would become enraged—to the point of harming me—when I disobeyed.

In those early years, when I would read the Word of God, I'd try to find all the words that encouraged me and gave me hope, while avoiding the ones that shone light on

letter I [ephesus]

areas that I hadn't allowed his loving discipline to adjust, granting repentance and enabling me to change. I was so scared of God being mad at me because of all the wrong things in my heart and life, so I would avoid the aspect of his fathering that included correction. Unfortunately, this stunted my growth and healing. I had to learn that it is only because he is a loving father that he examines the condition of our hearts and closely watches our lives. He does not want harm to come to us or to allow us to harm each other because of our brokenness.

His discipline is proof of his love, even when it hurts!

Before bringing correction, the Lord begins this letter to the church in Ephesus by assuring them he sees all their work and how they have performed it with zeal and diligence. He also understands the trials they have tirelessly endured. He commends them for these things first. What a precious example of how our good Father treats each one of us. He looks on the good works and quality of our lives and encourages us with compliments and recognition. He recognizes and praises our good deeds even when he is correcting and disciplining us. Our weaknesses and failures do not cancel out what we have done that is right and good. However, as a good and wise Father, he will not allow sickness or sin to remain, festering within us until it brings death to what is pure, but he will bring light to the places of darkness through an invitation into repentance.

Often, we labor and work diligently for God but forget about our intimate relationship with him, causing us

VII LETTERS

to work hard "for his Kingdom" even as we drift away from first love. We work out of duty not from a response of love. Any fruit from works that are not performed out of love's zeal will eventually wither and die; they spring up quickly as the result of a performance-based need for approval, and just as quickly pass away when we aren't appreciated or noticed.

> *Believers in every generation are in danger of becoming experts at ministry, simply performing tasks rather than deepening their passion for Christ. If they do, they will become like salt that has lost its saltiness (Matthew 5:13).*[2]

When we work in gratitude for his goodness and obey in humble service, God's love waters us, strengthens us, and restores us to run with him in all patience and diligence.

> *"In repentance and rest is your salvation, in quietness and trust is your strength…"* [Isaiah 30:15]

Repentance restores rest to us; it quiets our souls from the chaos of sin. Repentance causes us to be strengthened through his love and faithfulness as we trust in God. If I had allowed repentance to flow more freely in my life as a young believer, I would have had greater rest and been kept safe from many pits that the enemy dug for me. My avoidance of the gift of repentance, due to my belief that correction equaled separation from love, caused me to live far too long with heart issues and sin that produced chaos

---

[2] Onesimus Ngundu, "Revelation" in *Africa Bible Commentary*, ed. Dr. Tokunboh Adeyemo (Grand Rapids, MI: Zondervan, 2006), 1550.

letter I [ephesus]

and unrest. This holds true in our earthly relationships, especially in marriage. We avoid facing the hard issues and selfishness in our lives, believing that if they are exposed they will separate us from love. We become so familiar with unhealthy patterns and with tolerating diseased areas that they eventually infect every part of life.

My husband and I had a wake-up call about fifteen years into our marriage. We both realized that we had become not only familiar with areas that were not healthy in each another, but accepting and tolerant with allowing these deficiencies to affect and guide our interactions with one another. To humble ourselves and change seemed harder than continuing with the status quo we were accustomed to. If our relationship could be compared to a dance, changing things posed great risk if one of us to were to suddenly alter the steps to the dance we had learned. We would step on one another's toes and trip over each other. We had spent fifteen years forming and learning this dance—how could we risk changing it and having to learn the steps of relating to each other all over again?

In fear and trembling, we decided to let God and each other into those areas so we could change. And just as we feared, we spent a lot of time stepping on one another's toes while we learned a new "dance" together, but it was the best thing we ever did. Repentance brought rest and renewed love. We left the familiar for the unfamiliar and found renewed love and healthy interaction, allowing us to honor each other rather than hiding in interactions that avoided trigger areas.

VII LETTERS

In my book, *Finding Home: A Doorway of Hope*, I have a chapter titled "Familiarity: Thief of Intimacy." It discusses in depth how familiarity can lead us into dead works. This often happens in marriages where a couple do not take the time to put their spouse first. They busy themselves with all the tasks of life and family, forgetting that love is the fuel that keeps intimacy burning. We begin turning our relationship into a well-oiled machine that accomplishes a task rather than love that burns so bright that we work together out of zeal and passion for one another.

The church in Ephesus fell into the trap of familiarity and works, which caused them to lose the fire of love and intimacy. Can we ever become truly "familiar" with our God who is infinite, full of mysteries and wonder, limitless in love, and always creating? The closer we get to him, the more we realize how little of his nature and character we genuinely know. Instead, we find solace in the familiar and avoid the unknown that threatens to disrupt our sense of security. First love seeks to know its object more and more, continually discovering new layers of beauty. We can forever live in a "first love" experience with Jesus because each day the Spirit will reveal another hidden treasure, another facet of his infinite love and fascinating personality that fascinates us and changes us to become like him.

The Discipline of God

> *Repent and do the things you did at first. If you do not repent, I will come to you and remove your lampstand from its place.* [Revelation 2:5]

letter I [ephesus]

We live in a culture that gives assent to a pervasive (but incorrect!) belief that God does not bring consequences to his disobedient children. We see this mindset and belief manifested in parenting styles over the past couple of decades. The belief that turning a blind eye or refraining from discipline expresses love has failed to guide our children on the right path. There is significant benefit in knowing that wrong actions reap negative—and painful—consequences. Unfortunately, many young leaders in churches and other realms of society did not receive teachings about this truth. The idea that God's grace causes him to look the other way is damaging and dangerous. Because he is a loving Father, the Lord looks upon both the good and the bad (those things that will harm us or others). His discipline comes from, and is evidence of, his faithful love and kindness. It is grace that causes him to warn us that if we do not take his counsel and repent, we will suffer the consequences.

In his letter to Ephesus, God's mercy and grace warns them of what will happen if they do not heed his counsel: "I will come to you and remove your lampstand from its place."

Matthew Henry's commentary notes this regarding the removing of their lampstand:

> *If the presence of Christ's grace and Spirit be slighted, we may expect the presence of his displeasure. He will come in a way of judgment, and that suddenly and surprisingly, upon impenitent churches and sinners; he will unchurch them, take away his gospel, his ministers, and his ordinances from them, and what will the churches or the angels of the churches do when the gospel is removed?*

VII LETTERS

God's discipline and judgements are just and true; they are not at all separate from agape love. He is not being unjust because he will not allow his name and character to be misrepresented or violated by rebellion or hatred. He grants special protection and care to the churches that carry the truth of the gospel of Jesus Christ, but this can be lifted from a church that strays from the purity of the gospel. This was not only true in the first century. It is still true today. We must be careful and diligent to keep our message pure and our love burning strong as we obey the counsel of Holy Spirit and the Word of God. The Spirit of God spoke the Scriptures, and that counsel was written for every church and every age to come. God does not change; therefore, his Word and counsel are as true today as they were thousands of years ago. They do not expire or change with time or adapt to fluctuating cultural beliefs. The church in Ephesus is us and the counsel given to them is for us. The schemes of the enemy and the sins of man produce the same results, and we can be profoundly grateful for these letters and the counsel that has endured to lead us into truth and life.

> *Whoever has ears, let them hear what the Spirit says to the churches. To the one who is victorious, I will give the right to eat from the tree of life, which is in the paradise of God. [Revelation 2:7]*

God placed the tree of life in the middle of the Garden of Eden—a "terrestrial counterpart of the tree of life in the Eden above."[3] It is exciting and encouraging to know that as

---

3 "Revelation" in *The International Bible Commentary*, ed. F.F. Bruce (Grand Rapids, MI: Zondervan, 1986), 1601.

letter I [ephesus]

we overcome, we gain access to that glorious life! The Spirit is still speaking to the churches of today. As we ponder the counsel of the Lord to the church in Ephesus, we are receiving the counsel of the Lord for the church today. This will cause us to be victorious overcomers—giving us all the benefits of eternal life in paradise. What a joyous promise and reward!

LETTER TWO

Smyrna

> "To the angel of the church in Smyrna write:
> 'These are the words of him who is the First and the Last, who died and came to life again. I know your afflictions and your poverty—yet you are rich! I know about the slander of those who say they are Jews and are not, but are a synagogue of Satan. Do not be afraid of what you are about to suffer. I tell you, the devil will put some of you in prison to test you, and you will suffer persecution for ten days. Be faithful, even to the point of death, and I will give you life as your victor's crown.
> Whoever has ears, let them hear what the Spirit says to the churches. The one who is victorious will not be hurt at all by the second death. [Revelation 2: 8-11]

I love the declaration of who Christ is in the opening of this letter to the church in Smyrna! Jesus has been from the beginning and will be forever—he is the author and the finisher of our faith; He is from everlasting to everlasting; he is unchangeable; he forever stands as the great "I Am." He lived, died, and is now alive forevermore. He is the one who intercedes on our behalf; and he is the one who will stand as judge of every person at the end of time as we know it.

VII LETTERS

These words not only remind us of who he is, but they also serve to comfort us in times of distress and trials. This letter is not a letter of correction or call to repentance, but instead is a declaration of who he is and a warning of what is to come so that his beloved people might be prepared. It also includes a promise for those who endure suffering, "… even to the point of death."

The first thing that God shares in this letter is the difference between temporal prosperity and eternal riches. The church of Smyrna faced intense opposition due to the pervasive influence of emperor worship in the city, which was required by law. To resist meant imprisonment and possible death.[1] Though the believers may not have possessed a great deal of earthly goods, they were rich in the spiritual realm. Their treasures were stored up in heaven rather than earth, where rust and decay could destroy them.

You may not own large tracts of land or have six figures in your bank account, but you can be rich in the things that are eternal. That is a fortune that endures forever. When a man or woman dies in spiritual poverty, despite possessing great worldly wealth, all is lost.

A year after my husband and I were married we moved two thousand miles from home to go to Bible college, because we felt that God was calling us to the nations. During those years of study and working odd jobs to pay for college and living expenses, most of our friends back home were building careers and purchasing their first homes. When

---

1 Titus Kennedy, *The Essential Archaeological Guide to Bible Lands* (Eugene, OR: Harvest House, 2023), 328.

letter II [smyrna]

we finished Bible college, we felt that God still planned to train us in character and leadership, so we moved back to home and family in California. The first two years back, we struggled financially because we were not trained or experienced in any sort of career that would provide advancement and a stable salary. (This was in the 1980s, when such a thing was still a reality!) Most of our friends were starting families in their new homes, and accumulating the kind of resources that most young couples desire. Honestly, we felt ashamed that we didn't seem to have even basic worldly wealth. Our siblings and friends had established careers and purchased homes, and we knew they wondered why we seemed to be "behind" in setting up our future. Yet, as I look back, God was making us rich in spirit. He was more concerned about refining our character and hearts than he was about making us rich in temporal things. Of course, it is not wrong to have wealth, as long as you are not in spiritual poverty—but God choose a different path for us because of what he had planned for us. Had we been able to see ahead, it might have given us comfort since we would be moving more than remaining in one place. It is important to be at peace in whatever state of "riches" God has you in. But whether poor or rich, be sure to be spiritually rich.

The Suffering Church

Do not be afraid of what you are about to suffer. I tell you, the devil will put some of you in prison to test you, and you will suffer persecution for ten days. Be faithful, even to the point of death, and I will give you life as your victor's crown. [Revelation 2:10]

VII LETTERS

This could be written to believers in many parts of the world today. Our brothers and sisters in North Korea, China, Hong Kong, Egypt, and the Middle East have already faced imprisonment, suffering, and even death for their faith in Yeshua. Unfortunately, even in countries that are currently blessed with freedom, there will be more saints who will face this kind of suffering in the days ahead. What a comfort to know that there is a beautiful ending to suffering that includes a crown of victory. Though in our flesh we may experience fear and suffering, our spirits can "fear not" because no one can steal the promise that Jesus obtained for us on the cross.

I have many friends in mainland China and am aware of what they go through for the sake of Christ. I appreciate that this letter states "the devil will put some of your in prison to test you…" Just as the devil tested Job by putting him through great suffering—but he remained faithful amid his deep grief—I have heard many stories of my precious Chinese friends remaining faithful when separated from family, threatened, beaten, and experiencing horrific suffering. When I see them, I almost see the victor's crown already upon their heads—for they have already been found faithful in the face of death.

When I first heard about the Christian life and salvation through Jesus, I used to visit a local church and sit up in the balcony and listen. I wanted to know what this God was all about and the life that he offered. I was a young teenager who dealt with a lot of fear due to things I had

letter II [smyrna]

already experienced. One Sunday during my "exploration years," the church showed a series of movies about martyrs, one of whom was burned at the stake. This was followed by a challenge to the congregation to be willing to "suffer until death." Since I was not a believer yet and did not understand eternal rewards, I was gripped with fear and spent the next few years running from God, fearing that he would require me to face this kind of death; and I was sure that if it happened, my fear would cause me to deny him.

But when I finally encountered the depths of his love, I surrendered my life unreservedly. Now, when I read the verse, "Do not fear what you are about to suffer…" I am filled with a confident hope that if I am ever in a situation where I must suffer, even to the point of death, I know his love will overwhelm me, and I will be filled with the joy set before me. This deep work that has been done in my heart is only because of the kindness and power of his Spirit.

The call is for all believers to be fearless. Fearlessness is a product of fervent love and faith in God, which is fully present even during a severe trial. This is a major step of preparation for all believers....[2]

Of course, I do not want to suffer; but my heart is comforted that he is able to do what we do not understand for anyone who faces great suffering and death.

In January 2021, my younger brother died from Covid. He was in the hospital twenty-one days, and because of

---

2 Daniel C. Juster, ThD., *Passover: The Key that Unlocks the Book of Revelation* (Clarksville, MD: Lederer Books, 2011), 16.

VII LETTERS

rampant fear during that time he was not permitted any visitors, but I was able to have daily contact with him through texts. He was physically unable to talk due to lack of breath. Eventually his medical team placed him on a ventilator, but before that we wrote to each other several times a day. Although he was going through great physical suffering, every time I read a message from him he was focused on the faithfulness of God rather than his suffering. He spent most of his days worshiping through the physical pain and the panic that can engulf a person when they are unable to breathe. The worse his condition became, the shorter his texts—until his final one that merely stated, "Worshiping."

I believe Bob, too, received the victor's crown for remaining faithful to the point of death. Many of you reading this have suffered from the enemy's cruel attempts to cause you to give up, but God knew that you would overcome and receive the victor's crown. The victory is in remaining faithful to the end. Your suffering has not been in vain—your suffering has revealed to heaven and hell that you are a legitimate son or daughter of God. The enemy is convinced you will deny the Lord or turn away from trust; but you continued to stand and worship, and you did not deny him. There are many modern-day Jobs who will be revealed to us in eternity. Their story may not have been as dramatic as his, but they too were tested and they ultimately declared the faithfulness of God amid their trials.

<u>Do You Hear What I Am Saying?</u>

Whoever has ears, let them hear what the Spirit says to

letter II [smyrna]

> *the churches. The one who is victorious will not be hurt at all by the second death. [Revelation 2:11]*

Today the church needs to have ears to hear what the Spirit is saying. He is speaking to us out from these original letters, but I believe he is saying so much more. We must have ears that hear, because only his counsel and wisdom will lead us into all truth. We can ask the Spirit to give us ears that hear him clearly; he knows only too well how desperately we need his help.

> *Now if any of you lacks wisdom, he should ask God, who gives generously to all without finding fault, and it will be given to him. [James 1:5]*

We constantly need his wise counsel and, if we ask, we will receive it. Our Father will generously give it! Just as an earthly father does not find fault with his young son for asking questions, neither does our heavenly Father. Asking is one of the wisest things we can do as sons and daughters. Asking displays trust, humility, and teachableness. God gets so excited when we ask him something that he knows will benefit us. How often have parents looked at a child who impulsively did something foolish and had to say, "Why didn't you take the time to ask me?" Parents love to give wisdom, direction and counsel that brings blessings to their children.

The same is true with our Father in heaven.

When I began to live like a daughter before my heavenly Father, my life changed. The cycles I went through trying to figure out life through my thoughts, past experiences,

VII LETTERS

intellect, and fears was not getting me anywhere. I felt like a dog chasing my tail; lots of frantic activity and no forward progress. Throughout the Scriptures we read one story after another of God's advising his people to handle difficult circumstances in ways that are contrary to human logic.

In Judges chapter 7, we see that Gideon faced overwhelming odds in his battle against the Midianites. God's wisdom was to reduce his army by 90%, from 3000 to 300. How would three hundred men, led by an unlikely commander, defeat a vast and mighty enemy? Yet, God had a plan that would confound the wisest of leaders and the strongest of warriors, even though it was absolute foolishness to men.

My life has often been that way as well. In the year 2001, my husband was making more money than he ever dreamed possible, and we had just purchased our brand-new dream home. Only six months after buying it and moving our family of six, the Lord instructed us to have my husband leave his job, put our home up for sale, and move to another nation. In six weeks' time.

By our human understanding, this was foolish, perhaps even insane. How would we survive? If the house didn't sell quickly, how would we pay the mortgage? Why would we take our four children away from their extended family and close friends? We had more questions than answers.

I spend many nights during those six weeks arguing with God about his logic in asking us to do this. Finally, the day arrived for us to move. Our house had not sold, we

letter II [smyrna]

had almost no mission support raised, we only had temporary housing (which was a one-bedroom basement), and we didn't even have a visa to remain in the country for long. But we obeyed and as the days and weeks passed, every single concern was taken care of and every obstacle removed from our path. Our obedience, despite our reservations, resulted in the most significant shift we have experienced into fulfilling God's call on our lives. His ways surely are not our ways—that is why we need ears to hear!

We must posture our hearts and lives like those of children—sons and daughters who know, beyond a shadow of doubt, that they can trust in the love their mothers and fathers have for them.

When our heavenly Father speaks, we will listen humbly and attentively. We will trust in his love no matter his request or the circumstances before us—for he is a good, good Father.

LETTER THREE

Pergamum

"To the angel of the church in Pergamum write: 'These are the words of him who has the sharp, double-edged sword. I know where you live—where Satan has his throne. Yet you remain true to my name. You did not renounce your faith in me, not even in the days of Antipas, my faithful witness, who was put to death in your city—where Satan lives.

Nevertheless, I have a few things against you: There are some among you who hold to the teaching of Balaam, who taught Balak to entice the Israelites to sin so that they ate food sacrificed to idols and committed sexual immorality. Likewise, you also have those who hold to the teaching of the Nicolaitans. Repent therefore! Otherwise, I will soon come to you and will fight against them with the sword of my mouth.

Whoever has ears, let them hear what the Spirit says to the churches. To the one who is victorious, I will give some of the hidden manna. I will also give that person a white stone with a new name written on it, known only to the one who receives it. [Revelation 2:12-17]

It is worth mentioning that Jesus describes himself differently in each of the seven letters. When addressing the church in Ephesus, he was the one who holds the stars and walks among the lampstands. According to the letter, the

VII LETTERS

people are depicted as fallen, possibly asleep, and resembling falling stars.

To the church in Smyrna, he addressed himself as the first and the last. He also spoke of suffering, even unto death; so it is fitting that he described himself as the "last," since he is the victorious one over the last enemy—death—which will be placed under his feet.

Now, in the letter to the church in Pergamum, he describes himself as the one whose words are a sharp, double-edged sword. He then praises them for not renouncing their faith during a time of oppression, which had taken the life of a man of great faith, his "faithful witness" Antipas. John had already referred to Jesus himself as the "faithful witness" (1:5) and the example of our Lord's behavior during his trial and execution was undoubtedly a great encouragement for his people suffering persecution.[1]

This is a city that has sinned against God's word and violated his ways. Matthew Henry's commentary reveals insights about this passage of Scripture.

> *The church of Pergamos was infested with men of corrupt minds, who did what they could to corrupt both the faith and manners of the church; and Christ, being resolved to fight against them by the sword of his word, takes the title of him that hath the sharp sword with two edges. 1. The word of God is a sword; it is a weapon both offensive and defensive, it is, in the hand of God, able to slay both sin and sinners. 2. It is a sharp*

---

1   Adela Yarbro Collins, "Revelation, Book of," in *The Anchor Bible Dictionary*, Volume 5 (NYC: Doubleday, 1992), 705.

letter III [pergamum]

sword. No heart is so hard, but it can cut it; it can divide asunder between the soul and the spirit, that is, between the soul and those sinful habits that by custom have become another soul or seem to be essential to it. 3. It is a sword with two edges; it turns and cuts every way. There is the edge of the law against the transgressors of that dispensation, and the edge of the gospel against the despisers of that dispensation; there is an edge to make a wound, and an edge to open a festered wound to its healing. There is no escaping the edge of this sword: if you turn aside to the right hand, it has an edge on that side; if on the left hand, you fall upon the edge of the sword on that side; it turns every way.

The letter states, "I know where you live…" We can infer from the statement, "…where Satan has his throne" that this city was filled with corruption, rebellion, and temptations of every kind.

My family and I are familiar with this atmosphere. We have lived in the San Francisco Bay Area, in Portland, Oregon, and in the Washington, D.C. region. Each city is located in areas of great natural beauty, and they carry amazing redemptive promises; yet each city has been polluted by unmentionable sins, witchcraft, idolatry, corrupt power, and perversions, where good is called evil and evil good. To stand in faith, living amid such grievous sins, takes both great grace and great restraint. You must believe beyond what your eyes see and what your ears hear—and you must live above the temptations and pull of earthly opportunities and circumstances. The church in these types of places must learn to see God beyond the natural and to

VII LETTERS

live beyond what seeks to provoke even the most peaceful soul. Love must reach beyond the darkness to bring light and hope. Despite Satan creating a throne for himself in these cities (and cities like them), the church must become the living seat where the only true king, Jesus Christ, is enthroned. The church in Pergamum could relate to having to remain faithful while surrounded by debauchery. God is making sure that the believers in this place know that he has seen how they have remained faithful to his name in a place that is infamous for the profane and wicked. These "seats of Satan" will often become a seat of wicked and unjust rulership—though the world is Satan's "circuit court," certain cities or places may function as his throne or seat, where hell seeks to execute its evil practices. These places will usually have corrupt leadership and oppressive governments that strenuously oppose and even persecute religious believers. Hence, the letter to this church recounts their steadfastness as they witnessed the martyrdom of a fellow believer, Antipus, in their midst.

I believe that if the church in these modern-day Pergamum cities will keep their hearts, lives, and words pure, that they can, by the power and help of the Holy Spirit, topple the seat of Satan in their city and in turn, see the throne of Jesus established. This is how a city can turn around and be saved.

Once again, in this letter, God has a point of correction—he has something that has grieved his heart.

letter III [pergamum]

Nevertheless, I have a few things against you: There are some among you who hold to the teaching of Balaam, who taught Balak to entice the Israelites to sin so that they ate food sacrificed to idols and committed sexual immorality. Likewise, you also have those who hold to the teaching of the Nicolaitans. Repent therefore! Otherwise, I will soon come to you and will fight against them with the sword of my mouth.
[Revelation 2:14-16]

Having lived in many cities that might be referred to as "seats of Satan," I can tell you that these regions have pitfalls for the people of God to be aware of. The church in these areas must allow the Holy Spirit to keep them from the subliminal (or even obvious) influences at work.

We spent time in one city where witchcraft is overt and prevalent, and I saw how a spirit of manipulation and control operated within the churches. The desire to control is often a manifestation of the spirit of witchcraft, which seeks to control both the atmosphere and the lives it influences. Having a religious reaction requires less effort than seeking a godly response to demonic activity.

We also lived near a city filled with sexual perversion, and we encountered the churches in the region suffering deep relational divisions. The overt and pervasive sin in the culture offended believers, but rather than responding with love and prayer, they reacted with bitter judgement, and over time many people in the body turned on one another. I could cite many other examples.

VII LETTERS

Churches in these types of cities need their brothers and sisters from other regions to come and hold their arms up and battle alongside them.

Tragically, the younger generation may grow accustomed to the prevailing sins in a particular area. As they mature, they become familiar with the spiritual "atmosphere," and their consciences are hardened to the depravity of it as they are slowly enticed by the seduction of evil. We see this throughout the Scriptures as righteous kings and rulers married wives from nations steeped in the worship of other gods. Over time, these kings set up altars to foreign gods and even worshipped them.

Matthew Henry brings to light these pitfalls:

The filthiness of the spirit and the filthiness of the flesh often go together. Corrupt doctrines and a corrupt worship often led to a corrupt conversation.

He says that it can also lead to corrupt communion. God forbid that we bring corruption into our spirits, our doctrines, our worship, our conversations, and our communion together.

The letter goes on to call the church of Pergamum to "repent!" Repentance is not only for sinners, but also for the saints. Repentance is a gift that sets us free from slavery to sin. It is one of the greatest gifts we have been given. Before repentance, we were enslaved and chained to sins that led to decay and death. Repentance renews us, restores us, and gives us abundant life free from chains that hold us captive. We don't have to work for our forgiveness—as with

letter III [pergamum]

salvation, we ask for forgiveness and by grace we are forgiven. I am captivated by the verse in Philippians 2:12:

> *Wherefore, my beloved, as you have always obeyed, not as in my presence only, but now much more in my absence, work out your own salvation with fear and trembling.*

What is the significance of "work out your own salvation"?

Did our salvation come through our works or through grace? Of course, it was grace. Jesus took our sins upon himself so that we could be given the gift of salvation through him, since none of our works could have paid the penalty for our sin. Grace also gives the gift of repentance. This gift is not merely given for the day of salvation, but is available and profitable for those who are "working out their salvation" as they continue their journey. We must always rely on the grace by which we are saved, not turning to our works to earn any good thing. We must work out of love for God and our neighbors, without depending on our efforts to serve as some kind of religious penance for our sins. Salvation came to us by grace and every step of working out our salvation remains a gift of grace. When we fully grasp that everything we possess and are comes from grace, the righteous deeds of the saints remain untainted by human pride.

To this present time, many of us struggle with the concept of grace. We live in a performance-based society where only the most brilliant or the strongest succeed and win.

VII LETTERS

We are often overwhelmed with joy and humility by the gift of grace that is revealed to us at the time that we receive salvation. May it never be that we then begin to perform again! May we never revert to a work-based life that attempts to earn our position in society, in the church—or even in our future place in heaven. I am not writing against works—they are vital when they are the pure manifestation of the love and grace that we have been freely given. But works performed to earn a position are not pure and will, over time, defile us with selfish motives, pride, and entitled expectations. We will begin to work to receive, rather than work because we are loved and want others to know that love.

The Sword of His Mouth

> *Repent therefore! Otherwise, I will soon come to you and will fight against them with the sword of my mouth.*
> *[Revelation 2:16]*

What does the Lord mean when he says he will fight against them with the sword of his mouth? He was referring to the followers of a heretical sect that practiced falsehood and immorality.

We must first understand that compromise had been introduces to Israel through Balak (Numbers 22-24). The so-called "doctrine of Balaam" was a belief that a person could cooperate with the spirit of the world and still serve God. Some individuals had allowed this lie to replace the truth of the gospel of Jesus Christ, and this demonic doctrine had caused all God's people to engage in all kinds of

letter III [pergamum]

sins such as immorality, idolatry, and fornication. Purity had been exchanged for paganism.

Isaiah 11:4 calls the sword of his mouth, "the rod of His mouth"—or scepter of His mouth.

> *He will not judge by what he sees with his eyes or decide*
> *by what he hears with his ears;*
> *but with righteousness he will judge the needy, with*
> *justice he will give decisions for the poor of the earth.*
> *He will strike the earth with the rod of his mouth; with*
> *the breath of his lips, he will slay the wicked.*
> *[Isaiah 11:3(b)-4]*

This clearly depicts that the Lord will bring judgement through his spoken word. The church of Jesus Christ is always called to repent of the toleration of such sins and teachers of sin, which Balak represents in this letter.

In the mercy of Jesus, he is warning the church at Pergamum to repent (change their thinking) about the teachings of Balaam expressed through the Nicolaitans, which is referenced by early church fathers as a doctrine promoting pagan sexual permissiveness. This may be one of the groups attacked by Peter (2 Peter 2:2-3, 15) and Jude (Jude 11).[2]

If the people will not heed his words, those who remain unrepentant will be judged by the sword—the rod or scepter—of his mouth. The Word of God will execute judgement against all compromise and adherence to false doctrines. There cannot be mixture between the infallible

---

[2] E. M. Blaiklock, "Nicolaitans" in *The New Bible Dictionary*, ed. J.D. Douglas (Grand Rapids, MI: Wm. B. Eerdmans, 1979), 886.

VII LETTERS

Word of God and the corrupt doctrines of demons. The pure becomes defiled when compromise is introduced.

Even today, some Christian circles have allowed false teachers and teachings to be introduced. Years ago, Jeffrey and I had a dear friend who was struggling with homosexual attraction. He went for counseling at a local church, and the pastor introduced him to the notion that a Christian could engage in homosexual activity if they were born that way. For many years, our friend had stood against temptation, but after that day he gave full expression to the desires that had clutched at his soul. I can only pray that God has mercy on that "pastor" who led this lost sheep astray. The Word of God is clear, and we cannot pick and choose what parts we want to live by and what parts we will use to introduce new doctrines. To ignore this is to introduce the doctrine of Balaam.

Once again the letter says, "He who has ears, let him hear." Compromise begins allowing a "seat of Satan" in our lives and our cities. May we have ears to hear what the Lord is saying, then repent of compromise and live in a way that shows we honor his Word as pure and undefiled.

The Hidden Manna and The White Stone

> *To the one who is victorious, I will give some of the hidden manna. I will also give that person a white stone with a new name written on it, known only to the one who receives it. [Revelation 2:17, NIV]*

In the Book of Exodus God provided manna, a heavenly food source that sustained the Israelites during their letter III [pergamum]

forty years in the desert. The hidden manna that is spoken of here is a symbolic picture of Jesus, our Savior and Source of life, and the treasures of the Word of God. He is our sustenance as we wander through this life. He is our manna from heaven. Jesus called himself, "The Bread of Life"—our living bread. Those who eat that bread will have eternal life.

So, why is it hidden? Because it is only for those who believe. Those who do not believe will never taste the abundant feast of eternal life. Though many people spend their lives making sure they only eat healthy foods to help increase their longevity, unless a man or woman eats of this hidden manna, they will never enjoy life eternal. The unbeliever does not understand the hidden treasure within the believer that sustains them, for it is hidden within them.

I believe this hidden manna will be best understood at the marriage supper of the Lamb. We will partake of life-giving manna; the abundant power of life that defeated death and the grave.

At the last supper, when Jesus broke bread, he called it, "My body, given for you." Now, the church breaks bread often to remember the bread of life that was given and his blood that was poured out for us. We partake of the "manna of life" and await the hidden manna that will be given to us in heaven.

As we receive Christ, the hidden manna, we will be given a white stone. Bible scholars do not know why the imagery of a white stone is used, but there are several possibilities. First, in ancient Greece, a court jury would give a

VII LETTERS

white stone if the defendant was acquitted, or a black stone if the defendant was guilty. They would call this The White Stone of Acquittal. What beautiful imagery this offers— a white stone with a new name written upon it.

Another possibility is from a small object called a tessera. A tessera is made of wood, stone, clay, or bone. In ancient Rome, the Romans used tesserae as tokens that gave them admittance to special events. It was like a ticket to enter or "get in." There are several other possibilities, but one widely accepted explanation comes from the high priest's breastplate. The breastplate contained twelve stones, and each of these stones had the name of one of the twelve tribes of Israel. When the high priest would minister in the temple, he bore the names of God's chosen people while in God's presence. The white stone could be symbolic of the believer, who has been washed clean by the blood of Jesus, standing in God's presence.

Possibly the best explanation of the white stone has to do with the ancient Roman custom of awarding a white stone to the winner of a race or athletic competition. Much like the gold medal in our Olympic games, they received a white stone with their name inscribed upon it. This white stone awarded to the winner of the race or event would also serve as a "ticket of entrance" to a special banquet. Amazing!

What is this white stone symbolic of? Our acquittal! It represents the final judgement that renders our innocence. The One who judges the world with truth and righteousness gives a final verdict in favor of the one who has eaten

letter III [pergamum]

of the Bread of Life. I believe that this is a multifaceted symbol that depicts all these possibilities.

What a beautiful promise—we will receive a white stone of acquittal that gives us access and entrance to heaven after we have run the race and were found victorious!

When I was a young woman who had newly come to know the Lord, I dealt with an eating disorder. After years of struggling, I finally sought help through a Christian recovery center. I was away from my family for two months. It was a time of agonizing pain and loneliness, but it was necessary pain that enabled me to begin the process of healing and recognizing roots of unforgiveness, bitterness, shame, and self-hatred that had worked their way into my heart.

My last day at the treatment facility, my therapist took me for a walk around the desert landscape where the center was located. It was springtime in the desert and the cacti were in full bloom. I had never liked the desert, but to see it in spring bloom was breathtaking and appeared as an offer of great hope. During our walk, my therapist gave me the gift of a white stone in the shape of a heart. He wanted me to have it as a remembrance of the time my dry and desert season began to bloom. Today, decades later, I still have that stone to remind me of my acquittal from death—and as a reminder that I was given access to abundant life! It is my white stone that has my name written upon it, just like the one spoken of in the ending line of this letter: given to the one who receives it.

Yes, Lord, we receive it!

LETTER FOUR

Thyatira

"To the angel of the church in Thyatira write: 'These are the words of the Son of God, whose eyes are like blazing fire and whose feet are like burnished bronze. I know your deeds, your love and faith, your service and perseverance, and that you are now doing more than you did at first.

Nevertheless, I have this against you: You tolerate that woman Jezebel, who calls herself a prophet. By her teaching she misleads my servants into sexual immorality and the eating of food sacrificed to idols. I have given her time to repent of her immorality, but she is unwilling. So I will cast her on a bed of suffering, and I will make those who commit adultery with her suffer intensely, unless they repent of her ways. I will strike her children dead. Then all the churches will know that I am he who searches hearts and minds, and I will repay each of you according to your deeds.

Now I say to the rest of you in Thyatira, to you who do not hold to her teaching and have not learned Satan's so-called deep secrets, 'I will not impose any other burden on you, except to hold on to what you have until I come.

To the one who is victorious and does my will to the end, I will give authority over the nations—that one "will

VII LETTERS

> *rule them with an iron scepter and will dash them to pieces like pottery"—just as I have received authority from my Father. I will also give that one the morning star. Whoever has ears, let them hear what the Spirit says to the churches."* [Revelation 2:18-29]

Thyatira was a town of trade, a prosperous commercial center with many trade guilds, making it an important location on the Roman road from Pergamos to Laodicea.

During his second missionary journey, Paul met Lydia, a Thyatiran woman who was a trader of purple goods, in Philippi.

> *And on the Sabbath day we went outside the gate to the riverside, where we supposed there was a place of prayer, and we sat down and spoke to the women who had come together. One who heard us was a woman named Lydia, from the city of Thyatira, a seller of purple goods, who was a worshiper of God. The Lord opened her heart to pay attention to what was said by Paul. And after she was baptized, and her household as well, she urged us, saying, "If you have judged me to be faithful to the Lord, come to my house and stay." And she prevailed upon us.* [Acts 16:13-15]

It is not known for certain, but some believe perhaps Lydia or a member of her household brought the gospel of Christ to Thyatira, since there is no record of Paul traveling there. Whoever brought the good news of Jesus to this city was successful in establishing a church.

letter IV [thyatira]

<u>Eyes of Flaming Fire and Feet Like Fine Brass</u>

In the first line of the Letter to the church of Thyatira, Jesus is called, The Son of God. This title gives understanding to the reader that Jesus has the same nature as his Father. It goes on to reveal him as the one with "eyes of flaming fire."

What does this mean?

One meaning we find is in Revelation 2:23,

"... Then all the churches will know that I am he who searches hearts and minds, and I will repay each of you according to your deeds."

His eyes see and search the heart and mind of every man and woman. No one can hide what mediates on in their heart and mind. His eyes of fire pierce the secret places of our hearts like a man carrying a torch through a dark cave, bringing light to every crevasse. His eyes pierce the darkness with perfect understanding, insight, and knowledge of all people. His insight can purify and refine the willing heart.

What does it mean when we read, "His feet are like fine brass?" God goes forth or walks forward with caring provision for his church (his people) as he guides us in our journey of faith through life, accomplishing his purposes within us. His providence is constant, terrible, awesome, pure, and holy. His eyes see and his feet move to accomplish all that is right and true. Judgement comes from what he sees with perfect wisdom and then he acts or moves accordingly with perfect strength and consistency.

VII LETTERS

<u>I Know Your Deeds</u>

Once again, we witness the kindness of God who takes notice of what we are doing and how we are growing. Though there is correction and exhortation for alignment coming, he first wants us to know that he is proud of his people and sees our efforts and our good works. It's as though he is saying, "First things first. I love you; I see you and I am aware of all that you are doing." What a good Father. This assures us of his intimacy; he is closely acquainted with everything we do.

The Lord first recognizes that the church of Thyatira is charitable, not out of religious duty but out of love. They serve well; those who hold office within the church are commended for teaching and maintaining true doctrine and practices. He also mentions their faith, which is the key ingredient for all the charitable services, as well as their true doctrine and acts. Finally, he commends them for doing even greater works than they did in the beginning. This testifies of their growth and perseverance—and their growing faithfulness.

We all want these characteristics. We want our love, faith, patience, and service to grow and declare the faithfulness of God in our lives and cities.

<u>I Have This Against You</u>

Praise God for correction and for warning his people when we are being seduced or deceived. One reason I believe the Lord asked me to write this book is to bring awareness and alignment to today's church—his people

letter IV [thyatira]

of the twenty-first century. Though we live in a very different world with complex technology, global connections, and advances that would confound any person living when these letters were written; we have the same enemy who brings the same temptations and evil schemes.

Rather than merely read the letters and think how we are glad that these offences are not at work in our churches, it is time to study the letters and take inventory of areas that God may have something that he desires to correct in us. We can liken the words, "I have this against you…" to the words, "Son, listen to my wisdom so that you do not fall and lose your way." He is a loving Father, that is faithful to his covenant with the prophets and kings of old—promising that his covenant will remain from generation to generation. He was a father to Abraham and remains a father to us.

His words to the church in Thyatira bring this warning: "You tolerate that woman Jezebel, who calls herself a prophet."

Matthew Henry calls the ones that he is addressing, "Wicked seducers." As we know, the historical Jezebel was a wicked queen who had God's true prophets killed. In Thyatira, wicked seducers sought to draw men and women into idolatry and fornication while claiming to be prophets. They were divisive and usurped the place of true prophets and leaders (officers) within the church. Some of them even used the name of the Lord in their false teachings and perverse seductions. This was deeply grievous to the

VII LETTERS

Lord. These wicked seducers infiltrated the church family as well. Not all of God's servants listened or bowed to their deceptions—but they tolerated them (most likely to avoid backlash).

> *I have given her time to repent of her immorality, but she is unwilling.*

In God's great patience, he gave those who had been seduced into this sin time to repent of their immorality, but they refused to do so. This makes their punishment even more terrible. So why is the church in Thyatira being held to account for the sins of those who engaged in this immorality? Most likely because it had crept into the church and since those practicing such things had not repented when given the opportunity to do so, it was now the church's responsibility to remove (excommunicate) them.

We are told in Matthew 18:6,

> *But if you cause one of these little ones who trusts in me to fall into sin, it would be better for you to have a large millstone tied around your neck and be drowned in the depths of the sea.*

By allowing those who are practicing the sin of Jezebel to remain, even after being given sufficient time to repent, they are putting a stumbling block in the way of other believers, especially young believers. We see that today in our churches and will most likely see an increase of this as "wicked seducers" have infiltrated our schools, our media, our government and in every area of society. Children are

letter IV [thyatira]

now being raised with immorality being called pure and purity being called evil. We need to be as wise as serpents and gentle as doves in dealing with those who come through our doors—especially when it comes to putting them in leadership. The pure and matured gift of discernment is a much-needed gift to the church, accompanied by mature leaders who can lead people to repentance and possess the wisdom to know when "enough is enough."

Why is the church of Thyatira rebuked for the sins of those who engage in the sins of Jezebel? Once again, let's look at what Matthew Henry has to say about this:

> *They had not, as a church, civil power to banish or imprison her; but they had ministerial power to censure and to excommunicate her: and it is probable that neglecting to use the power they had made them sharers in her sin.*

God has given us biblical protocol for dealing with a person or group of people who are engaging in sinful activity within our churches. Matthew 18:15-17 brings us godly wisdom for dealing with sin.

> *"If your brother or sister sins, go and point out their fault, just between the two of you. If they listen to you, you have won them over. But if they will not listen, take one or two others along, so that 'every matter may be established by the testimony of two or three witnesses.' If they still refuse to listen, tell it to the church; and if they refuse to listen even to the church, treat them as you would a pagan or a tax collector."*

VII LETTERS

If today's church would adhere to this standard Jesus gave us, we would have far more unity and greater purity. This process allows the person who is in sin to repent; first privately, if they are willing. Far too often I have seen many people talking "about" another's sin (or perceived sin) rather than following the instructions given to us in Matthew 18. Gossip does not lead a brother or sister to repentance—love, compassion and truth is the way to the cross. Is it easier to have a leadership meeting about an individual's struggle, or even deliberate sin, than to get face to face with them? Believe me, I have been guilty of this as well. The better way will lead them to repentance, or at least provide the opportunity for repentance. If they are not willing to hear truth or turn from their sin, then the proper thing to do is to remove them before they cause another to fall.

The words in Matthew 18 are not merely a suggestion; they are a principle that gives authority to those who obey them. Jesus taught these to his disciples and followers to help them know how to walk out sin with a brother or sister that is sinning. If we followed this wisdom, unity would be preserved, and peace would be established within the church. Gossip, tolerance, avoidance or a "cold shoulder" will merely create dissention and chaos. Those reactions also allow a place for the sin to spread to others.

If we are to look at sin like a weed in a garden, rarely does one weed come up without spreading its roots underground and causing many weeds to spring up from beneath what is seen; eventually choking out the plants that bear

letter IV [thyatira]

true fruit. When we bring sin into the light, we create an opportunity for it to be pulled up (roots and all) through the willing act of repentance. It may take more than one step, but the desired outcome is a true repentance that will cause that brother or sister to be set free and bear fruit. If they will not repent, it is better to have them leave than to spread sin, disunity, and chaos throughout the congregation.

Jezebel and Babylon

So I will cast her on a bed of suffering, and I will make those who commit adultery with her suffer intensely, unless they repent of her ways. I will strike her children dead. Then all the churches will know that I am he who searches hearts and minds, and I will repay each of you according to your deeds. [Revelation 2:22-23]

These verses not only speak of this "spirit of Jezebel" but also of the end-time Babylon. The name "Babylon" is derived from the Akkadian word **babilu**, which means "gate of god." This is a counterfeit of God's eternal city. Babylon is a place that practices opposition to the rule of God by world powers. It also conveys a metaphor; the exile of God's people from the land of blessing. In Revelation 18 we see how Babylon falls in one hour from a great power to a place of destruction—even eternal destruction.

After this I saw another angel coming down from heaven. He had great authority, and the earth was illuminated by his splendor. With a mighty voice he shouted: "'Fallen! Fallen is Babylon the Great!' She has become a dwelling for demons and a haunt for every impure

VII LETTERS

spirit, a haunt for every unclean bird, a haunt for every unclean and detestable animal. For all the nations have drunk the maddening wine of her adulteries.

The kings of the earth committed adultery with her, and the merchants of the earth grew rich from her excessive luxuries."

Then I heard another voice from heaven say:

"'Come out of her, my people,' so that you will not share in her sins, so that you will not receive any of her plagues; for her sins are piled up to heaven, and God has remembered her crimes. Give back to her as she has given; pay her back double for what she has done. Pour her a double portion from her own cup. Give her as much torment and grief as the glory and luxury she gave herself. In her heart she boasts, 'I sit enthroned as queen. I am not a widow, I will never mourn.'

Therefore in one day her plagues will overtake her: death, mourning and famine.

She will be consumed by fire, for mighty is the Lord God who judges her. "When the kings of the earth who committed adultery with her and shared her luxury see the smoke of her burning, they will weep and mourn over her. Terrified at her torment, they will stand far off and cry:

"'Woe! Woe to you, great city, you mighty city of Babylon! In one hour your doom has come!'

"The merchants of the earth will weep and mourn over her because no one buys their cargoes anymore— cargoes of gold, silver, precious stones and pearls; fine linen, purple, silk and scarlet cloth; every sort of citron wood, and articles of every kind made of ivory, costly wood, bronze, iron and marble; cargoes of cinnamon and spice, of incense, myrrh and frankincense, of wine

letter IV [thyatira]

and olive oil, of fine flour and wheat; cattle and sheep; horses and carriages; and human beings sold as slaves. "They will say, 'The fruit you longed for is gone from you. All your luxury and splendor have vanished, never to be recovered.' The merchants who sold these things and gained their wealth from her will stand far off, terrified at her torment. They will weep and mourn and cry out:

"'Woe! Woe to you, great city, dressed in fine linen, purple and scarlet, and glittering with gold, precious stones and pearls! In one hour such great wealth has been brought to ruin!'

"Every sea captain, and all who travel by ship, the sailors, and all who earn their living from the sea, will stand far off. When they see the smoke of her burning, they will exclaim, 'Was there ever a city like this great city?' They will throw dust on their heads, and with weeping and mourning cry out:

"'Woe! Woe to you, great city, where all who had ships on the sea became rich through her wealth! In one hour she has been brought to ruin!' "Rejoice over her, you heavens!

Rejoice, you people of God! Rejoice, apostles and prophets! For God has judged her with the judgment she imposed on you."

Then a mighty angel picked up a boulder the size of a large millstone and threw it into the sea, and said: "With such violence the great city of Babylon will be thrown down, never to be found again. The music of harpists and musicians, pipers and trumpeters, will never be heard in you again. No worker of any trade will ever be found in you again. The sound of a millstone will never be heard in you again. The light of a

VII LETTERS

> *lamp will never shine in you again. The voice of bridegroom and bride will never be heard in you again. Your merchants were the world's important people. By your magic spell all the nations were led astray. In her was found the blood of prophets and of God's holy people, of all who have been slaughtered on the earth."*
> *[Revelation 18:1-24]*

Once again, we see a Babylon-type world forming before us that stands in opposition to God and has introduced a toleration toward spiritual corruption. We see world leaders calling what is good, evil and what is evil, good while forcing those evils into laws and new societal norms. The place referred to in Revelation 18 may be an actual city, and John's original readers in the first century would likely have thought of Rome; however

> *...[Babylon] has taken many forms since then and is in fact a picture of the human race in rebellion against God, as we find it in our own culture. Revelation's visions of cosmic collapse have spoken to every generation of readers, but they have even more relevance to an age of global environmental pollution and destructive capabilities that transcend those of any previous age. The visions of Revelation are always up to date...*[1]

We cannot identify "end-time Babylon" with certainty, but it definitely refers to governmental (political) and economic atrocities and a wicked spirit of rebellion and arrogance. The destruction and judgement against this

---

1   "Revelation, Book of," in *Dictionary of Biblical Imagery*, ed. Leland Ryken, James C. Wilhoit, and Tremper Longman III (Downers Grove, IL:InterVarsity Press, 1998), 715.

letter IV [thyatira]

end-time Babylon and the Jezebel spoken of in the letter mirror each other. Death and destruction will come upon her.

Yet, even now, God gives time for those who have been enticed with spiritual corruption and for those who release edicts that oppose God, to repent. But this is only a "period of time" that is set by God alone. We also see churches that are not only tolerating this corruption but calling it holy. They have been seduced by the spirit of the world—Babylon and Jezebel—to the point of retranslating scripture to fit their immoral practices. The appetite of the flesh has replaced genuine hunger for God.

We must pray like never before for our children, our churches, our governmental leaders and for the citizens of our nations. We now see clearly how this Babylonian spirit has infiltrated even our most sacred places. Schools now say that we do not have rights to decide what they teach our children, even our youngest children. Many even say that if one of our children are to reveal that they are being taught biblical truth that opposes the narrative of the "woke" that it is a hate crime against those who have chosen an alternate lifestyle. How tragic that men and women (even children) who were created in the image of God's likeness now can't even identify their gender as male or female but demand that we learn new "pronouns" to identify them such as "they." This is a terrible robbery of dignity, honor, and the astonishing intricacy God put within each of us.

VII LETTERS

Even amid such atrocities and defilement of God's nature and creation, this chapter in the Book of Revelation gives encouragement to those who kept themselves pure and undefiled from the compromises and violations of God's ways.

Deep Secrets or Dark Secrets

> *Now I say to the rest of you in Thyatira, to you who do not hold to her teaching and have not learned Satan's so-called deep secrets, 'I will not impose any other burden on you, except to hold on to what you have until I come.' [Revelation 2:24-25]*

Though God brings correction to the church in this region for tolerating Jezebel and all of those who are practicing the perversions that this spirit has introduced, he also encourages and brings comfort to those who have not wavered from truth. "Satan's so-called deep secrets," as they are referred to, were presented to the people as new revelation or deep spiritual secrets. The truth is that these were demonic perversions and deceptions that introduced compromise and straying from the truths that Jesus brought forth. It would be more fitting to call them dark secrets rather than deep secrets.

We see these "revelations of deep secrets" continue today in churches and religious organizations. You can drive around any large city and see churches with names such as Church of Scientology, Unitarian Church, Center for Spiritual Living, Mediation Center—and the list goes on. All of these (and many others) believe that they have

letter IV [thyatira]

been enlightened to a deeper mystery (secret) that is diverse and inclusive. Unfortunately, their inclusiveness has made a place for the Jezebel spirit to run rampant with all kinds of perversions that stray from God's holy and pure truth.

My husband and I had a dear friend who attended Bible college with us and was one of my husband's groomsmen in our wedding. We were unaware at the time but later learned that he was struggling with same-sex attraction. He battled this temptation for many years—even going through Youth With A Missions discipleship training, Bible college, faithfully attending a Spirit-filled church, and surrounding himself with Christian relationships. But he secretly had a separate group of friends that were not believers, and a separate life that fed this unnatural sexual desire. He chose to not "come out from among them." He secretly continued to compromise in his heart to the point of being susceptible to deception. Finally, he turned to a pastor at a local Episcopalian church and was told that his desires were not only normal, but healthy! This pastor then counseled him to stop fighting his "natural" desires and to embrace his "design." Immediately after this meeting our friend turned away from all his Christian friends, left our church, and began a relationship with a male friend whom he later married. I know that there are Episcopalians who love the Lord and believe the whole Bible (without compromise), but this is one of many denominations that has not only tolerated Jezebel but embraced her teachings—dark secrets and mysteries—as truth. Now homosexual

VII LETTERS

individuals can be ordained in many denominations that still call themselves Christian.

We cannot compromise God's truth for the sake of making a place for sin to thrive or temptations of the flesh to become acted upon. We must hold to the truth that was given to us by the teachings of Jesus and the complete Word of God. God encourages the Church of Thyatira to hold on to what they have until he comes. What they have is the Words of Jesus that speak truth. They have salvation through Jesus, and they have grace by which they are save. With this letter, they also have the counsel of God to move forward without compromising or tolerating demonic practices or receiving demonic revelation. They have truth and that truth sets them free. We too have this counsel and truth so that we can be free from all entanglements with Jezebel and her practices.

A Promise of Victory and Authority

> *To the one who is victorious and does my will to the end, I will give authority over the nations— that one 'will rule them with an iron scepter and will dash them to pieces like pottery'—just as I have received authority from my Father. I will also give that one the morning star. Whoever has ears, let them hear what the Spirit says to the churches.* [Revelation 2:26-29]

These words and promises—to the one who is victorious and does my will to the end—may be for now as well as for the time to come "when believers sit down with Christ on his throne of judgment, and join with him in trying, and

letter IV [thyatira]

condemning, and consigning over to punishment the enemies of Christ and the church" (Matthew Henry). We want to be a victorious church who continues to do his will to the very end. As we walk in his will, we walk in his victory and authority both now and at the time that all the nations are judged.

"I will also give that one the morning star."

Jesus is the morning star who brings light, hope, grace and glory. It is interesting that in Isaiah 14:12 Lucifer is also called the morning star,

> *"How you have fallen from heaven, O morning star,
> son of the dawn! You have been cast down to the earth,
> you who once laid low the nations!"*

Before the fall of Lucifer, he was exquisite and powerful. When he rebelled against God, he became a falling star that will one day no longer be seen. Christ is the most beautiful and most powerful; his light and power will never end or fade away for there is no darkness within him.

> *There will be no more night. They will not need the light
> of a lamp or the light of the sun, for the Lord God will
> give them light. And they will reign for ever and ever.
> [Revelation 22:5]*

When the new heavens and the new earth are revealed, there will be no need for any alternative light source because Jesus, our Morning Star, will be our source of light for all eternity. We will be given the morning star! What a beautiful promise and astounding revelation of the greatness of our God.

LETTER FIVE

Sardis

"To the angel of the church in Sardis write:
'These are the words of him who holds the seven spirits of God and the seven stars. I know your deeds; you have a reputation of being alive, but you are dead. Wake up! Strengthen what remains and is about to die, for I have found your deeds unfinished in the sight of my God. Remember, therefore, what you have received and heard; hold it fast, and repent. But if you do not wake up, I will come like a thief, and you will not know at what time I will come to you.

'Yet you have a few people in Sardis who have not soiled their clothes. They will walk with me, dressed in white, for they are worthy. The one who is victorious will, like them, be dressed in white. I will never blot out the name of that person from the book of life, but will acknowledge that name before my father and his angels. Whoever has ears, let them hear what the Spirit says to the churches.'" [Revelation 3:1-6]

Sardis was an ancient city in Lydia, on the banks of Mount Tmolus. According to historical accounts, Sardis held the title of chief city in Asia Minor (modern-day Turkey) and was the first city in the region to embrace John's preaching.

VII LETTERS

Sardis was a busy center for the traffic of goods and ideas between Mesopotamia and the Greek Ionian settlements. Sardis served as a crossroad of trade and gained a reputation as the perfect meeting point for the exchange of ideas, beliefs, customs, knowledge, and new insights. Over the years, it went from a thriving city that received the gospel of Jesus Christ to a place where death and defeat swallowed up its prosperity and people. It faced defeat in battles and even experienced massive earthquakes that literally caused mountains to collapse and the earth to bury its citizens.

At the time John wrote, Sardis was a very ancient city, "becoming the capital of the Lydian kingdom in the 7th century BC but existing centuries before that."[1] The letter to that church may be the most grievous letter of any of them, as it describes their "dead state." They were in danger of losing everything. Christianity did persist there for some time after Jesus's message to them, but today there are no known Christians in the small, modern city now known as Sart. There is no record of how many people possibly repented and turned back to the Lord, allowing his counsel and correction to resurrect what God desired for the city and her inhabitants.

The Deception of Reputation

> *These are the words of him who holds the seven spirits of God and the seven stars. I know your deeds; you have a reputation of being alive, but you are dead.*
> *[Revelation: 3:1]*

---

1 Titus Kennedy, *The Essential Archaeological Guide to Bible Lands* (Eugene, OR: Harvest House, 2023), 337.

letter V [sardis]

Once again, we see the Lord reveal himself in a way uniquely appropriate to the letter and those receiving the words found within. Jesus is referred to as "him who holds the seven spirits of God and the seven stars" to begin this letter. Jesus has the seven spirits—the Spirit without measure—fully perfect and limitless. He gives a different portion, or measure, of his Spirit to the seven churches, bringing each one unique abilities of strength, the power through grace to do what God has asked of them and an anointing to carry out their assignments in a unique fashion—making them effectual in growth and longevity. The Lord does not remove their portion, but it can be forfeited by those to whom it is given if they will not appropriate it.

Why did the Lord reveal himself in this way? The purpose was to remind the church of Sardis that they possessed all the necessary resources to thrive, grow, and be faithful to their assigned tasks. They had the Holy Spirit and his appointed graces providing them the resources needed to be a living, thriving church. An angel and angelic ministers had been assigned to this church to help them in every way. Jesus was holding them accountable for all they were given, and for the misuse of their gifts. Though they had a reputation for being alive and thriving, they were dead and languishing—and in danger of losing what they had been given if they would not heed his counsel and apprehend the help provided for them. His message was urgent.

> *The church partook of the character of the city, whose name was almost synonymous with pretension unjus-*

VII LETTERS

> *tified, promise unfulfilled, appearance without reality, confidence which heralded ruin. Quite evidently compromise with its pagan environment had so eroded the witness of the church in Sardis that it was a Christian church in name only. Revival and repentance are urgently called for; otherwise there is no future for the church.*[2]

I believe that we, as churches and individuals that make up the global church, share the responsibility to steward all that we have received. We have all been apportioned gifts, talents, abilities (graces) and strengths that are to be used to glorify the Lord and further his Kingdom here on earth. Angels have been assigned to us to help us remain faithful and zealous in all that we do. They minister to us, send us messages and battle against powers and principalities, rulers of darkness and demons that have been sent to oppose us. We want to be careful to not only acknowledge all that we have been given but to faithfully use it for the sake of his name. Just as the church in Sardis was apparently doing, we can also forfeit that which we've been given. This is one of the most tragic deaths there is—more grievous than the death of the body is the death of the life given to someone by the choice to forfeit it.

We are not judged on our reputation but rather on our lives, our hearts, and our faithfulness to steward all that we have been given.

---

[2] F. F. Bruce, "Revelation" in *The International Bible Commentary*, ed. F. F. Bruce (Grand Rapids, MI: Zondervan, 1986), 1603.

letter V [sardis]

<u>Wake Up</u>!

With each previous letter that we have explored, God opened the letter with words of approval regarding what they are doing right and encouragement for moving forward. This is not the case in this letter to Sardis. Right off the bat, it is a rebuke—a warning and a powerful command. His tone and "get right to the point" wording remind me of those times when one of my kids would do something or was about to do something that could bring them great harm. As a mother, I almost always corrected my children with what I'd call gentle authority. I would sit them down and ask them if they knew what they had done wrong, and I would always tell them how proud I was of all that they did right while still correcting their wrongdoing (sometimes with appropriate discipline and other times with mercy). I distinctly remember a few times while raising my kids—especially as teenagers—when I knew one of them was not listening or using the wisdom and teachings that we had instilled in them. One time I came face to face with a very deliberate moment of rebellion that I knew would have terrible consequences if my teen was not stopped. It was a "WAKE UP!" moment that did not come with the gentle reminders of how proud I was or with encouragement for the days ahead. I spoke words that were clear, direct, precise, and said with absolute authority as a parent. It was one of those "911" parenting moments where there was no time to soften the blow. It was forceful and emphatic, just as the Lord is in this letter.

VII LETTERS

To speak this way is loving! It is not a reaction from bitterness or offense, but correction springing from passionate and unwavering love and protection. God wanted to make sure his words were heard and understood. He was telling them their reputation did not align with their reality—"You are not alive but you are dead!" He was calling for them to wake up from deception into truth. Their spiritual lives were at stake and the Father wanted them to live.

Jesus's strong words to "wake up" are especially interesting when we note that many sudden catastrophes struck Sardis at night or when the people were not on alert, such as two major earthquakes, the assassination of the king who resided in the city, usurpation of the throne by the Greek king Gyges—and many years later a secret attack by the Persians.[3]

The Applause of Men

Strengthen what remains and is about to die, for I have found your deeds unfinished in the sight of my God.
[Revelation 3:2]

The church in Sardis was well spoken of and appeared to be not only alive, but thriving in every way. They were most likely growing, active, vibrant and exciting to those who attended or who passed by. If they were a church today, their social media site would have been booming with likes and followers. Yet, there was something that God saw the bystander was not seeing. Something was lacking in their

---

3   Titus Kennedy, *The Essential Archaeological Guide to Bible Lands* (Eugene, OR: Harvest House, 2023), 338.

letter V [sardis]

deeds—what was that? Let's look at 2 Timothy 3 to explore what God may have been seeing.

> *But mark this: There will be terrible times in the last days. People will be lovers of themselves...having a form of godliness but denying its power.*
> *[2 Timothy 3:1-2, 5, NIV]*

Hypocrisy: The practice of claiming to have moral standards or beliefs to which one's own behavior does not conform; pretense.

How often do we see a famous person with a reputation for good deeds and kindness, and then later find out that they are abusive, controlling, and untrustworthy? Far too often, I fear. It is easy to "act a part" before an audience and give wealth before the eyes of men while all along causing great pain and sorrows to those who know them privately and personally. This is hypocrisy. It appears the church of Sardis became very good at acting the part of a strong Christian and probably very skilled at playing that part before the eyes of onlookers. No man, no woman, and no ministry can hide from God what is the truth beneath to the exterior. He knows the sincerity of heart and the surrender to his Spirit. Power comes from the Spirit of God, therefore, apart from his Spirit, there is only a form of godliness that is void of power. If we are void of power, then we are void of life and true fruitfulness. Those who reported about this church were probably viewing the performance of men who had "good form." Maybe Sardis was the "Christian Hollywood" of the Bible days—but God

VII LETTERS

was not impressed or fooled. Yet, he loved them enough to issue this strongly worded letter, hoping they would turn from their wicked ways.

Let's look at the context of the verses from 2 Timothy 3 quoted above:

> *But mark this: There will be terrible times in the last days. People will be lovers of themselves, lovers of money, boastful, proud, abusive, disobedient to their parents, ungrateful, unholy, without love, unforgiving, slanderous, without self-control, brutal, not lovers of the good, treacherous, rash, conceited, lovers of pleasure rather than lovers of God—having a form of godliness but denying its power. Have nothing to do with such people. They are the kind who worm their way into homes and gain control over gullible women, who are loaded down with sins and are swayed by all kinds of evil desires, always learning but never able to come to a knowledge of the truth. [2 Timothy 3:1-7, NIV]*

I recently heard a minister talking about how many in the church of America have become a "people of appetite and not of true hunger." We have so much around us, we can unintentionally develop a habit of continually satisfying our appetite without ever truly experiencing what it is to hunger for God. Here in America, where food is readily available, we will say, "I'm starving." And yet what that means is that my flesh is craving to be fed something that will satisfy my appetite. It may have only been an hour since our last "appetizer" but suddenly our desire for something that comforts our cravings is demanding to be

letter V [sardis]

satisfied once again. By continually indulging ourselves, we have forgotten what true hunger feels like.

Spiritually speaking, this can be true as well. Many believers have developed a lifestyle of satisfying their appetite for "a form of godliness" while never actually experiencing true hunger for God that causes us to seek him with our whole hearts. We can live a lifestyle that is satisfying our appetite through continual spiritual music, podcasts, prophetic words, edifying quotes, zoom calls, etc. There is always a way and opportunity to quickly satisfy the appetite of the Christian's soul.

Paul understood hunger for God. Having spent much time in prison, I am sure that he lacked any source to fill his soulish appetite and came to the point of desperate hunger that drove him to seek God with all his heart and soul and mind. If we do not learn to hunger, we could be at risk of being one of those that Paul talks about when he says, "There will be terrible times in the last days. People will be lovers of self, of money (etc.) …having a form of godliness but denying its power." Maybe we should say, "***Having a form of appetite but denying genuine hunger.***"

I pray for the body of Christ, that we will not be found satisfied with temporary cravings, comforts, or mere forms of godliness, but that we would eat what is good and delight in the Lord.

Why spend your money on what is not bread, and your labor on what does not satisfy? Listen, listen to me, and eat what is good, and you will delight in the richest of fare. [Isaiah 55:2]

VII LETTERS

We see this in the letter to the church in Sardis (Revelation 3). The leaders of this church had a reputation for being hungry and alive, but God called them "dead" and strongly exhorted them to "Wake up!" They did not hunger and thirst for God, but they satisfied themselves (and their parishioners) with worldly things. They turned their affections towards satisfying their appetite instead of seeking true hunger and thirst for God and all his ways. The affections of men and the reputation that caused them to give a good appearance before men had become what satisfied their appetite.

God, save us from such a fate, and keep us from the temptation of seeking to be satisfied with all the riches that the world has to offer in exchange for the hunger of knowing your Son.

An Invitation to Repent

> *Remember, therefore, what you have received and heard; hold it fast, and repent. But if you do not wake up, I will come like a thief, and you will not know at what time I will come to you. [Revelation 3:3]*

God is reminding his church of the portion of his Spirit that they received, as well as the message of the gospel of Jesus they heard at first. Later, we will read a letter to the church of Laodicea where they are called to "return to their first love." When the men and women of Sardis first heard the message of the gospel, their hearts burned to serve him and know more about him—but now, they were merely a shell of the people who had first responded to him. They

letter V [sardis]

had stopped being watchful over their own souls and over one another, allowing sin and compromise to enter. They exchanged their righteousness for the good rapport of men.

The love and mercy of God was reaching for them and calling them to come back to the message that they heard at first—and to their first love (though he does not use this language). He is pleading with them to remember all he gave them and to hold on to it. I see this like a picture of a man hanging onto a ledge with one hand. It is a desperate moment as he is losing his grip and ability to hang on. It is as though they are being reminded that they have another arm that they can grab hold with and pull themselves up. But their second arm is busy with the things and is not concerned with that they are about to lose what was given them.

In my early years as a believer, I quickly found myself in leadership roles within the church. I truly was not ready for these positions, but I had a "reputation for being alive and equipped." I had found validation and identity in leadership roles and the approval of man more than true spiritual maturity. When I realized that my ability to hang onto the leadership roles, were costing me my health because of my deep, unresolved brokenness, I fought desperately to push down the pain to "keep my reputation." God quickly rescued me from my own foolish choice and asked me to humble myself and seek healing. I needed genuine life and maturity, not merely a form of these virtues. I stepped down from all leadership roles and spent the next three years letting the Lord heal me, mature me, and help me to find my

VII LETTERS

identity in him alone. I truly woke up and lived for the first time. What a joy to finally not be grasping to hang on to a reputation, but to be able to live a reality of being redeemed.

This was the offer that the Lord gave the church in Sardis. They could hang onto a reputation of being alive (all the while, being dead) or they could repent and take the time for God to redeem and restore them into genuine awakening and resurrection. The most heartbreaking part of this story is that those in Sardis never repented, and the church and the city ultimately faced annihilation.

A Pure Remnant

Yet you have a few people in Sardis who have not soiled their clothes. They will walk with me, dressed in white, for they are worthy. [Revelation 3:4]

God never forgets the faithful—even if they are few. These precious few kept themselves clean and set apart from the vile practices in this city that had compromised most of those who called themselves believers. In this letter, God does not forget to mention them and to give them a promise to keep their hearts hopeful and encouraged. They will walk with me, dressed in white. The white garment that is referred to in this verse is the Roman garment called a *stola*. It was the staple garment of the married woman in ancient Rome. To wear a stola signified that a woman was married. What a beautiful promise of being the Lord's bride. This letter promises them the garments of a bride, for they are legitimate and will be married in covenant to the Lord.

letter V [sardis]

This imagery also gives us a clue to what soiled garments mean. If the white garments depict a married woman, then soiled garments would signify an adulterous woman—one who has given herself to another and broken covenant relationship. How deeply grievous.

In Genesis 18, Abraham pleads for Sodom, asking God if there are fifty righteous, will he save it? Then he asks if there are thirty, then twenty, and finally ten. Each time the Lord says that if there are even ten righteous, he will save the entire city. These few, who had not soiled their clothes were the dam that was holding back judgment on Sardis. I can only imagine that over time, these righteous ones left to find a company of believers that held the same values and convictions as they did—the purity of covenant. Once the true remnant was gone, most likely, that is when judgment came.

My husband and I live in the Portland, Oregon region and I truly believe that what is holding back God's judgment in our region is the righteous remnant faithfully seeking God. We are part of the senior leadership at a church in downtown Portland and I have seen among the people we labor with a deep commitment to remain pure and undefiled, and to live in covenant relationship with the Lord and each other. Our worship is pure, the prayers are passionate, and the sacrifice is costly. I moved here with my family from the San Francisco Bay Area, which has similar depravity within its borders and on its streets. You will find a faithful remnant holding back the judgment of God from coming

VII LETTERS

upon that region as well. The few provide mercy for the many. What a compassionate and long-suffering God we serve!

The purity of one outweighs the depravity of many—ushering mercy for the many where judgment is deserved.

The One Who Overcame Holds the Book of Life

The one who is victorious will, like them, be dressed in white. I will never blot out the name of that person from the book of life, but will acknowledge that name before my Father and his angels. [Revelation 3:5]

Jesus, our victorious King, who has overcome sin and death, will be dressed in white. Everyone who believes in Jesus and has been washed in his blood will be clothed in white linens, symbolizing his righteousness granted to them. His white garments reveal his purity, perfection, holiness, and glory. We are clothed in the purity of his attributes because he is our eternal Bridegroom. It is grace that has wrapped us in clean garments—not our righteousness or purity, but his alone.

I am overcome by the beauty Matthew Henry describes regarding this verse in his *Commentary*.

The purity of grace shall be rewarded with the perfect purity of glory. Holiness, when perfected, shall be its own reward; glory is the perfection of grace, differing not in kind, but in degree.

"Glory is the perfection of grace"! I found myself reading these words over and over, hoping my mind would

letter V [sardis]

perceive the weight of them. There is a greater grace that is even now beginning to wrap around the people of God. It is a grace that covers our shortcomings and a grace that gives authority based on the Lord's perfect purity. The reliance and reality of the depth of God's grace is becoming a glory resting upon his church. As the world gets darker, his light becomes brighter, causing our eyes to see the spots and wrinkles we still possess. And yet, his grace and glory cover our nakedness and his perfect purity and glory cover us and make us clean. This truth regularly leaves me overcome and bowed low in humility these days.

He also holds the Book of Life in his hands. Because we have received this gift of grace and salvation, our names have been written in the Book of Life—never to be blotted out. Jesus will confess our names before our heavenly Father and before the angels.

I had a beautiful encounter several years ago that had an amazing moment of grace and the Book of Life in it. My husband Jeffrey and I had received a call while we were traveling that his mother was in the hospital, and the doctors were not giving any hope for her survival. We needed to get on a plane right away if we wanted to see her before she passed. Jeff's mom had resisted any attempts to share the gospel with her over the years and, though she was a wonderful lady and loving mother, she had not received the gift of salvation through grace. We could not understand why, since all her family knew Christ.

VII LETTERS

As we made the plane reservations, our friend and host gathered us in her kitchen and said, "Let's ask Holy Spirit what is stopping your mom from receiving Jesus as her Savior." So, we closed our eyes and asked this simple but profound question.

As we waited, our host asked us, "Did your mom have blonde hair with curls as a child?"

We answered, "Yes."

"Did she live in a place with green pastures and rolling hills?"

"Yes, she lived on a hundred acres in the hills of Sonoma County, California."

Our host paused a moment, then asked, "Did she lose a beloved pet when she was about eight to ten years old? I see her praying in a grassy field for a pet that she dearly loved but her pet died, and she decided she would never turn to God again."

Jeffrey knew immediately that it was her horse. It had died when his mom was around eight years old, and she loved it deeply.

At that point we asked Holy Spirit what we were to do about this. We suddenly knew that Jeffrey, who was her first born as well as the first "born again" member of his family, needed to stand in the gap for her. He invited the Holy Spirit and angels to minister comfort to her heart and let the compassion of the Lord deal with her anger about the horse's death. He released the pain and broke the vow that she would never pray to God again. As this happened,

letter V [sardis]

we received a text message from one of Jeffrey's family members at the hospital with his mom, and they said she was "talking to someone who was not there." She even asked Jeffrey's dad to move out of the way because she wanted to see the man behind him. No one else could see "the man," but they realized she was seeing the Lord.

During our time on the plane, as we traveled to be with her, I went into an encounter where I saw Jesus holding the Book of Life. He confessed her name before the Father and the angels, and I saw a white feather pen write her name in gold in this beautiful Book. I immediately knew that she had accepted the Lord. As soon as the plane landed and I took my phone off "airplane mode," I received a message from our friend who had prayed with us, telling me she had an encounter where she saw the name of Jeffrey's mom written in gold in the Book of Life!

We were overjoyed and overwhelmed by the mercy and goodness of God. We led our family in worship that day in her hospital room, and in one of her final conscious moments, she told me she was ready to go to heaven. She had received the grace of salvation and promise of heaven—despite having never served Jesus during her earthly life. Amazing grace!

How he longs to show grace and mercy to people! He does not take pleasure in bringing judgment; he deeply desires to extend mercy out of his love and compassion. If only the world knew of this perfect purity that clothes us in grace and glory. If only. Let us see the Book of Life filled

VII LETTERS

with names no one expected to be in it as we pray that even those who have stubbornly resisted him will come to see their need of the life Jesus offers.

<u>Whoever Has Ears To Hear</u>

> *Whoever has ears, let them hear what the Spirit says to the churches. [Revelation 3:6]*

Once again, we read the same closing words that we have read in previous letters. The Spirit is still speaking to the church today.

I often find myself reading the Book of Proverbs lately. It is a book of a father's wisdom to his precious son. It gives wisdom, counsel, and warning alike. When Solomon was set as king, the Lord asked him what he desired. Rather than ask for wealth, power, success, or a long life, he asked for the "wisdom to lead this great people." Because he asked for that which pleased the Lord, God not only answered him but added to him even the things that he did not ask for: wealth, power, success, and a long life.

Oh, that we would desire for the wisdom to lead people into God's righteousness and his ways more than temporal blessings. God would gladly add to us the "lesser" things, such as wealth and long, fruitful lives. We have his Spirit with us who is willing and desiring to give us wisdom and understanding that will cause us to bear much fruit. His wisdom will keep us from deception, and give us Spirit-led insight so we do not lead people according to human understanding. His wisdom is a light for our path and

letter V [sardis]

guidance when we do not know what to do or what to say. We must remember that our thought are not his thoughts, and our ways are not his ways—his thoughts and ways exceed even the wisest brilliance of mankind. His thoughts don't always make sense to us, but they are always fruitful and bring success.

Consider the march around Jericho. Any commander of an army going into battle would mock the strategy of marching around a city wall for six days, then on the seventh day go around seven times, and on the seventh time releasing a shout. Human understanding tells us to raise up an army trained and equipped to overcome their enemy. And yet, God sends the children of Israel to face the enemy with no training and no weapons—only obedience. They had ears to hear the instructions of the Lord, the walls fell, and the city was taken.

One of my greatest desires is to see the body of Christ ask for ears to hear the wisdom of God once again. I see so many strategies based on human understanding and people following teachings that tell them how to defeat the enemy standing in their way. But, like young David before Goliath, even a youth can ask and receive wisdom that will defeat an enemy. We do not need human strength, but heavenly wisdom. We need ears to hear.

LETTER SIX

Philadelphia

"To the angel of the church in Philadelphia write:
'These are the words of him who is holy and true, who
holds the key of David. What he opens no one can shut,
and what he shuts no one can open. I know your deeds.
See, I have placed before you an open door that no one
can shut. I know that you have little strength, yet you
have kept my word and have not denied my name. I
will make those who are of the synagogue of Satan, who
claim to be Jews though they are not, but are liars—I
will make them come and fall down at your feet and
acknowledge that I have loved you. 10 Since you have
kept my command to endure patiently, I will also keep
you from the hour of trial that is going to come on the
whole world to test the inhabitants of the earth.
I am coming soon. Hold on to what you have, so that
no one will take your crown. The one who is victorious
I will make a pillar in the temple of my God. Never
again will they leave it. I will write on them the name
of my God and the name of the city of my God, the new
Jerusalem, which is coming down out of heaven from
my God; and I will also write on them my new name.
Whoever has ears, let them hear what the Spirit says to
the churches.'" [Revelation 3:7-13]

VII LETTERS

Philadelphia of Lydia, located at modern Alasehir, Turkey, was on the Imperial Post Road, an important military and trade route. Its name means "love of a brother." Philadelphia was about twenty-six miles from Sardis. The path between the two cities was a path of trade and communication from the harbor of Smyrna and from Lydia. It was a vital route from Ephesus to the east. This route was the main "communication line" coming from Rome (the Imperial communication).

The region around Philadelphia suffered frequent earthquakes; the walls of the city had many cracks from the numerous shakings it experienced. For this reason, most of the people lived outside the city as farmers in rural homes and villages. In A.D. 17, a large earthquake several cities in the region, and Philadelphia suffered damage.[1]

Emperor Tiberius helped Philadelphia rebuild after this devastating earthquake. The citizens showed their gratitude by changing the name of the city to Neocaisarea—meaning "New Caesar."

Philadelphia was set apart from other cities because of these characteristics: it was "the missionary city"; its people always lived in fear of disaster or what they called "the day of trial." However, in the first century there seems to have been no imperial cults or pagan temples in the area, so there were few problems with syncretism in the church.[2]

---

[1] Titus Kennedy, *The Essential Archaeological Guide to Bible Lands* (Eugene, OR: Harvest House, 2023), 340.

[2] Titus Kennedy, *The Essential Archaeological Guide to Bible Lands* (Eugene, OR: Harvest House, 2023), 341.

letter VI [philadelphia]

Open and Shut

These are the words of him who is holy and true, who holds the key of David. What he opens no one can shut, and what he shuts no one can open. [Revelation 3:7]

The Lord begins this letter by identifying himself as "...him who is holy and true, who holds the key of David. What he opens no one can shut, and what he shuts no one can open." He is declaring his holiness, sovereignty, and authority through these words. The reference to the key of David is from the Messianic prophecy Isaiah 22:22.

I will place on his shoulder the key to the house of David; what he opens no one can shut, and what he shuts no one can open.

Regarding the church of Philadelphia, the open door is God's declaration that they are a gateway of missionary service to the cities in that region. The church of Philadelphia was to go forth and carry the gospel of Jesus Christ to the region, the cities of Phrygia. Out of his sovereignty and holiness, he has spoken and declared this door or gateway open.

Jesus the Messiah holds the key to the house of David, which is a governmental key, and he controls the opening and closing of doors of opportunity for his people in Philadelphia (and for all his people everywhere).[3] He is governmentally unlocking a door of blessing and protection over the believers in this city. Even as they live amongst a people plagued by fear of shakings, they do not need to

---

3 Daniel C. Juster, ThD., *Passover: The Key that Unlocks the Book of Revelation* (Clarksville, MD: Lederer Books, 2011), 19.

VII LETTERS

fear for they will be protected: his blood is upon the doorpost of his church.

I was born and raised in California, in "earthquake country," so I understand living with the continual awareness of potential "shaking." I went through many earthquake drills in school during my childhood. And I've been through countless small earthquakes, and two major ones that resulted in property damage and fatalities. Today, the fear of wildfires because of drought conditions have trumped the fear of earthquakes, but as believers, there is a promise over his church in California (and regions like this) of his protection and blessings. Many godly people live there as present-day missionaries, influencing the state amidst wickedness and compromise. They choose to remain in the land as keepers of the promise who bring the gospel to the lost. We must remember, God did not come for the well, but the sick. We must not curse or question why people remain in regions such as this, but pray for them; for their strengthening and encouragement, and for their families to be protected from the evil one.

I love what Matthew Henry has to say about the opening and shutting of the Holy One:

> *He opens. He opens a door of opportunity to his churches; he opens a door of utterance to his ministers; he opens a door of entrance, opens the heart; he opens a door of admission into the visible church, laying down the terms of communion; and he opens the door of admission into the church triumphant, according to the terms of salvation fixed by him.*

letter VI [philadelphia]

He shuts the door. When he pleases, he shuts the door of opportunity and the door of utterance, and leaves obstinate sinners shut up in the hardness of their hearts; he shuts the door of church-fellowship against unbelievers and profane persons; and he shuts the door of heaven against the foolish virgins who have slept away their day of grace, and against the workers of iniquity, how vain and confident soever they may be.
The way and manner in which he performs these acts, and that is absolute sovereignty, independent upon the will of men, and irresistible by the power of men: He openeth, and no man shutteth; he shutteth, and no man openeth; he works to will and to do, and, when he works, none can hinder.

No one can hinder! What an amazing promise and declaration for the global church. Maybe we should consider, when we are dealing with situations we think are hindrances, that they may be doors shut by God. We should focus on the open doors and open hearts that are ready to receive salvation. We must seek the Lord's wisdom rather than trying to knock down closed doors in our own strength. He will give us insight as to how we are to pray, and even if doors have been shut because of the stubbornness of people's hearts, God is able to open any door when it is his time.

Matthew Henry continues:
These were proper characters for him, when speaking to a church that had endeavored to be conformed to Christ in holiness and truth, and that had enjoyed a wide door of liberty and opportunity under his care and government.

VII LETTERS

<u>You Have Kept My Word</u>

> *I know your deeds. See, I have placed before you an open door that no one can shut. I know that you have little strength, yet you have kept my word and have not denied my name. [Revelation 3:8]*

God is encouraging his believers by assuring them he knows all their deeds. He knows that they have accessed the open door under his care and government, even while facing many adversaries. Facing adversaries does not equal closed doors; it is merely a part of living in a world contaminated by sin and by individuals who have aligned their lives and actions with the evil one.

"I know that you have little strength…" There is a wide-open door, and they have grace in their weakness to keep his word and preach Jesus as Messiah.

> *As with all the churches, the Lord knows the strengths and weaknesses of the Philadelphian church…Continuing the idea of opening and shutting, he declares that he has opened a door for them, and because he is the one who has opened it, no one else will be able to shut it.*[4]

Additionally, there is a way to gain strength despite our weaknesses, and that is to grow in grace.

> *But grow in the grace and knowledge of our Lord and Savior Jesus Christ. To him be glory both now and forever more! Amen. [2 Peter 3:18]*

---

4   Onesimus Ngundu, "Revelation" in *Africa Bible Commentary*, ed. Dr. Tokunboh Adeyemo (Grand Rapids, MI: Zondervan, 2006), 1552.

letter VI [philadelphia]

God does not give us grace because of our good works, but to help us do the work he has set before us. As we apply grace to the "little strength" we have, it grows. This is how we overcome adversity and accomplish keeping his word and honoring his name. But how do we grow in grace?

- By Keeping His Word.

He acknowledges that the Church of Philadelphia has kept his word—this is a key to their growing strength as they grow in grace. We must receive strength and edification from his Word, both through personal studies and by sitting under (as well as reading works by) anointed teachers.

- By Declaring His Name.

We were saved by grace through Jesus Christ, his shed blood and torn flesh and his death and resurrection. He alone is our grace. We grow in grace as we continue to acknowledge and declare his salvation and redemption in every part of our lives. We declare it to those who are lost, and we declare it as his heirs of salvation. This act causes the grace by which we were saved to grow and expand in our lives—bringing us strength. This is truly "Amazing grace!"

Your Enemies Will Fall At Your Feet—Confessing, Jesus as Lord

I will make those who are of the synagogue of Satan, who claim to be Jews though they are not, but are liars—I will make them come and fall down at your feet and acknowledge that I have loved you. Since you have

VII LETTERS

> *kept my command to endure patiently, I will also keep you from the hour of trial that is going to come on the whole world to test the inhabitants of the earth.*
> *[Revelation 3:9-10]*

Many claim to worship God and be his people, but because they merely mouth loyalty to God but do not honor him with their hearts and lives, they are shown to be liars by their actions. In verse 8 we see that men have been coming to the true believers to mock and harass, claiming that they are the genuine people of God—the Jews. Yet, their profession is merely in words and not deeds. They claim their Jewish rights and yet deny the true God. They seek to intimidate and bring accusation again those who have become born again through the belief that Jesus is the Messiah.

Through the millennia, down to this present time, many Gentile believers have added "fuel to the fire" by teaching that the church has replaced Israel, and God's promises no longer apply to the Jews. Such "supersessionism" (or "replacement theology") claims that the Jews are no longer God's chosen people. This is a doctrine of demons that denies much clear biblical teaching, and seeks to negate the beautiful scriptural promise noted in Ephesians 2:14-15 that the Lord will create "one new man" and there will be unity, peace, and reconciliation between all believers, both Jews and Gentiles. Asher Intrater writes,

> *As the Gentile Christians humble themselves and recognize their Jewish roots, the blindness on the Jews*

letter VI [philadelphia]

that keeps them from receiving Yeshua as Savior will be removed, and the Jews will be saved...History bears out that when a nation with Gentile Christians accepts and embraces the Jews in a positive way, many Jewish people come to believe in Yeshua.[5]

God is declaring that the Jews will see that believers in Messiah Yeshua have obtained a special blessing and unique favor through God's tremendous mercy. They will come to the point of acknowledging that they have been wrong in their accusations and will desire to experience the love that is poured out upon these believers. They will even seek to become a part of the Church of Yeshua as they encounter this uncontainable love that reveals that he is indeed their long-awaited Messiah.

I believe we are coming upon those days. We will see jealousy arise in the hearts of those who "claim to be Jews" and yet have actually been part of the synagogue of Satan as they have vehemently denied their true Messiah and accused his followers of blasphemy and apostasy.

Yeshua's church will demonstrate his agape love like never before. This love-revival will reveal the oneness that Messiah prayed for his people to receive in John 17:20-23, creating a holy jealousy within the unbelieving hearts of the Jewish people, and removing their blindness, as Asher noted. They will acknowledge their error and turn their lives over to Yeshua. They will run to the Messianic Jews whom they have mocked and accused, and they will run

---

[5]   Keith (Asher) Intrater & Dan Juster, *Israel, the Church, and the Last Days* (Shippensburg, PA: Destiny Image, 2003), 146-147.

VII LETTERS

to the Gentiles—who have been grafted in—and acknowledge that those people also know the truth. These men and women will understand that the true Israel is the body of Jesus Christ, made of Jews and Gentiles. Israel is a nation, but it is also a people, and those people are the believers in Yeshua—both Jew and Gentile. As they witness this love and oneness that they have never known, their hardened hearts will become soft and pliable. The favor on God's people will be undeniable and greatly desired.

Then, in verse 10 we read these words:

Since you have kept my command to endure patiently, I will also keep you from the hour of trial that is going to come on the whole world to test the inhabitants of the earth.

Verses 9 and 10 carry such promise, not only to the historic church of Philadelphia but to the end-time church. I deeply believe that there are two distinctions that will be seen in God's end-time people that was present in the church of Philadelphia: the agape love of God and brotherly love for each other. This is the fulfillment of the prayer of Jesus in John 17:20-23:

"My prayer is not for them alone. I pray also for those who will believe in me through their message, that all of them may be one, Father, just as you are in me and I am in you. May they also be in us so that the world may believe that you have sent me. I have given them the glory that you gave me, that they may be one as we are one—I in them and you in me—so that they may be brought to complete unity. Then the world will know

letter VI [philadelphia]

that you sent me and have loved them even as you have loved me.

Remember, the name Philadelphia means "brotherly love." The only way that we can truly display the oneness and love that causes the world to know that Jesus is Messiah is through his glory that rests upon the people he so deeply loves. A family will come forth through the Son who was given as a ransom for the sins of mankind.

Then, there is a glorious promise in verse 10, "…I will also keep you from the hour of trial that is going to come on the whole world to test the inhabitants of the earth." He will keep us from the hour of trial that comes upon the whole world. Though we do not fully know what this keeping will look like or how it will be manifested, it surely will come upon us in the time of testing and trial. We will be kept safe from it. This is a reward for not denying Christ or serving other gods throughout the past trials that we have endured. Our posture, even today, is gaining for us a great reward that will keep us from enduring the hour of trial and testing that comes upon the inhabitants of the earth.

Matthew Henry describes it like this:

Those who keep the gospel in a time of peace shall be kept by Christ in an hour of temptation. By keeping the gospel, they are prepared for the trial; and the same divine grace that has made them fruitful in times of peace will make them faithful in times of persecution.

It is a divine and sovereign "keeping" that causes us to be both fruitful and faithful to the very end, in the hour of peace as well as the hour of persecution. Once again, the world will witness his people walking in the midst of the fiery furnace—with its heat turned up—without being burned. They will see the fourth Man in the furnace and acknowledge that the God we serve in the only true God. His people will go through this time like Shadrach, Meshach, and Abednego. They did not bow in the hour of peace, and they were kept in the hour of persecution.

<u>Secure Your Crown and Hold Fast</u>

I am coming soon. Hold on to what you have, so that no one will take your crown... [Revelation 3:11]

Just as the Church of Philadelphia was counseled to "hold on to what they had" or to hold fast to what they had; I believe we are in an hour to "hold fast." As we hold on to or hold fast to Christ and all that we have received from him in this hour, he will hold us in the days ahead. Those who have continued to hold fast to Christ in the day of peace will be held by him in the day of persecution. Let's look at some verses that talk about holding fast.

Let us hold fast the confession of our hope without wavering, for He who promised is faithful...
[Hebrews 10:23]

We are to hold onto our confession of hope without wavering, knowing that he who promised is faithful to accomplish all that he has said.

But examine everything carefully; hold fast to that which is good... [1 Thessalonians 5:21]

letter VI [philadelphia]

We are to discern between good and evil and hold to what is good and right according to the standard of Christ.

You shall fear the Lord your God; you shall serve Him and cling (hold fast) to Him, and you shall swear by His name. [Deuteronomy 10:20]

We are to cling to him and serve him no matter what is happening to us or around us. We must hold fast to him and hold fast to the fear of the Lord over the fear of man.

Then his wife said to him, "Do you still hold fast your integrity? Curse God and die!" [Job 2:9]

We are to hold fast to our integrity amid suffering. Just as Job would not curse God when he was suffering, we are to hold onto the conviction and confession of God's faithfulness without becoming divided or compromising our integrity in Christ.

…but Christ was faithful as a Son over His house—whose house we are, if we hold fast our confidence and the boast of our hope firm until the end. [Hebrews 3: 6]

We are the dwelling place of Christ, and he is faithful to his people. Therefore, we must hold fast to our confidence in him and declare our confident hope in his faithfulness until the very end.

For we have become partakers of Christ, if we hold fast the beginning of our assurance firm until the end. [Hebrews 3:14]

We are to hold fast to our confession that Jesus is our high priest, seated at the right hand of his Father. We hold fast to the confession that Jesus is the Son of God!

VII LETTERS

> *Therefore, since we have a great high priest who has passed through the heavens, Jesus the Son of God, let us hold fast our confession. [Hebrews 4:14]*

When we were born again, we became convinced that Jesus Christ is our Savior and we confessed him as such. We do not know what the future holds, but we can make the choice to hold fast to what we have experienced of his mercy.

> *So, remember (hold fast to) what you have received and heard; and keep it, and repent. Therefore, if you do not wake up, I will come like a thief, and you will not know at what hour I will come to you. [Revelation 3:3]*

No one knows the moment that they will take their final breath. Therefore, we just hold fast to all that we have learned, believed, received, and heard—keeping it always in our minds and hearts. That which we hold fast to or keep now will become a reward in the days ahead, where we find that God himself holds fast to us and keeps us in his perfect care.

As we hold fast to what we have confessed with our mouths, we will surely gain every promise and reward that is ours through Christ Jesus. We know that there will be those who do not maintain their crowns because they did not hold fast to his ways and his faithfulness in the time of preparation. They did not cling to Christ or cling to the hope of his faithfulness. They confessed Christ while becoming more and more enraptured by their crown than their King.

letter VI [philadelphia]

<u>His Name Will be Written Upon You</u>

The one who is victorious I will make a pillar in the temple of my God. Never again will they leave it. I will write on them the name of my God and the name of the city of my God, the new Jerusalem, which is coming down out of heaven from my God; and I will also write on them my new name. [Revelation 3:12]

Those in Christ, the ones who served him no matter the cost, will achieve victory and will not have any defeat or shadow of sin or death remaining upon them. Those who held onto Christ as their beginning and end will stand as a memorial to his name for all eternity. Just as they stood for Christ, they will be remembered for carrying his name and he will write his name upon them for all to see.

These victorious ones will also have the name of the city of God, the New Jerusalem, written upon them. The New Jerusalem is the Church of God—which will come down out of heaven. During their lifetime, these saints edified the church through their acts of service and sacrifice. They helped to expand, equip, teach, lead, purify, and mature the church of God during their time on earth. Like handmaidens or bridesmaids prepare the bride to stand before her bridegroom, these victorious ones have prepared the Bride of Christ, adorning her with every spiritual gift and eternal treasure.

What a joy it is to know that the Lord remembers our deeds and our sacrifices that we have offered during our lives. Though that is not why we served, it is a direct benefit and honor given to those who served the church of God.

VII LETTERS

I am reminded of women who take part in the old tradition of "quilting circles." Each person works on a single square or patch of a blanket, applying her unique creativity and expertise to produce beauty that—in collaboration with others—becomes a beautiful, enduring pattern. When the individual squares are joined, the end result is a beautiful quilt.

The New Jerusalem is like a heavenly quilt designed by God to be presented at the end of days. Each person, through the ages, will have worked on their piece with integrity, beauty, and wonder. Those pieces will be joined by our magnificent Creator, each detail fashioned precisely and becoming part of a wondrous city coming down from heaven. And the name of this city will be written upon you, because you were a part of the company throughout the ages who fashioned it.

He will also place upon us "his new name." There are many thoughts and opinions of what this refers to, but whatever it is, we know it will represent the fullness of who he is to his bride. The ones who kept their lamps lit while waiting for him through the long night (Matthew 25)—those who bought oil to maintain their lamps—and those who did not turn away when the night tarried. These will be the ones who will bear his name just as a bride takes the name of her bridegroom when they enter into the marriage covenant.

This line in verse 12 always reminds me of the morning after my wedding. My newlywed husband Jeffrey and

letter VI [philadelphia]

I woke up early in our San Francisco hotel where we were catching a flight to our honeymoon destination in Hawaii. When we approached the airline counter to check in, the representative looked at my ticket and said, "Good morning Mr. and Mrs. Pelton." In that moment I realized that I now carried Jeffrey's name. The joy that filled me was unlike anything I had ever known. I now had his name as part of my life—I was called by that name. I will never forget it because the fulfillment of my greatest dream was realized in that very moment. I have never known a moment of such absolute joyful fulfillment in an unexpected single moment. This is what I believe it will be like when we receive his name written upon us.

> *Whoever has ears, let them hear what the Spirit says to the churches. [Revelation 3:13]*

Once again, the Lord is giving a charge at the end of the letter. It is a letter for those who will hear and obey. The letter includes promises, blessings, and counsel. It says, "Whoever has ears." We all have ears; therefore, this letter is for all men and women who have been given spiritual ears to hear. Let us hear what he is saying. Today the Spirit is still speaking to the churches and the letters to the early churches have wisdom and counsel for the end time church.

We are listening.

LETTER SEVEN

Laodicea

"To the angel of the church in Laodicea write: 'These are the words of the Amen, the faithful and true witness, the ruler of God's creation. I know your deeds, that you are neither cold nor hot. I wish you were either one or the other! So, because you are lukewarm—neither hot nor cold—I am about to spit you out of my mouth. You say, "I am rich; I have acquired wealth and do not need a thing." But you do not realize that you are wretched, pitiful, poor, blind and naked. I counsel you to buy from me gold refined in the fire, so you can become rich; and white clothes to wear, so you can cover your shameful nakedness; and salve to put on your eyes, so you can see.

'Those whom I love I rebuke and discipline. So be earnest and repent. Here I am! I stand at the door and knock. If anyone hears my voice and opens the door, I will come in and eat with that person, and they with me. To the one who is victorious, I will give the right to sit with me on my throne, just as I was victorious and sat down with my Father on his throne. Whoever has ears, let them hear what the Spirit says to the churches.'"

[Revelation 3:14-22]

VII LETTERS

Laodicea, situated in Asia Minor, was part of the Roman Empire's region known as Phrygia, near present-day Denizli, Turkey. Located on a major trade route, Laodicea was a wealthy city, known for textile production (including a soft, raven-black wool), a famous medical school (known especially for ophthalmology and its production of eye-salve), banking, and a complex water system.[1]

The seven letters were given to John during the reign of the Roman emperor Domitian—the first Roman emperor to declare himself a god during his reign (previous emperors had only been declared deities after their deaths). This man was notorious for persecuting individuals who refused to worship emperors and dynastic families. The persecution included preventing people from trading and owning property. It is possible that some believers, accustomed to the wealth they enjoyed in Laodicea, divided their loyalties between the emperor and the Lord to avoid losing their social status, their possessions, and possibly their lives.

Our Amen!

> *These are the words of the Amen, the faithful and true witness, the ruler of God's creation. [Revelation 3:14]*

What an interesting way for the Lord to address himself: "the Amen." What does this mean?

He is the final word, the great agreement, the fullness of every purpose and fulfillment of every promise. He is the "Amen" to his never-changing Word, will, and ways.

---

1 Titus Kennedy, *The Essential Archaeological Guide to Bible Lands* (Eugene, OR: Harvest House, 2023), 345.

letter VII [laodicea]

I believe he addressed himself this way to the church of Laodicea to emphasize his true identity and the sincerity of his message. It is a serious and final warning from our merciful Judge and Savior; the Amen.

"...the faithful and true witness." These words describe God as the witness of everything he has done for man, and everything man has done for God. Our faith is witnessed by God, his hosts, and all who have gone before us. It is a witness or testimony to heaven. Both angels and demons alike witness and recognize our belief and God gives witness and testimony regarding our faith. God is also a witness—a faithful witness—of his dealings with man. All creation witnesses his faithfulness, his truth, his grace and goodness, his patience and endurance. Every good and perfect gift God gives to his creation is witnessed by both heaven and hell. There is no case against him.

"...the ruler (and beginning) of God's creation." He was and forever will be the creator of heaven and earth. He rules over the beginning and the end of all things. He is the author and finisher of our hope and salvation and the firstborn from the dead. He is over all creation. Amidst great evil, his grace and mercy enable the progression of time in human history— but it is God alone who decides the end of the age. He is patient, not desiring for any man to perish, but for all to come to the knowledge of his dear Son.

There are moments in the lives of men and women who have gone astray where the Lord, in his marvelous lovingkindness, issues a correction with an "amen." There

VII LETTERS

is deep seriousness in these moments—for lives are being held in the balance of heaven and hell. He often does this to those who have shown lukewarmness and lived on the fence of indecision. He will come and say, "You must decide between covenant or compromise, obedience or rebellion, heaven or hell." The church of Laodicea was hanging in that place of indecision, and the Lord's patient, loving, and stern warning demanded a decision from them about who they would serve.

Make Up Your Mind

> *I know your deeds, that you are neither cold nor hot. I wish you were either one or the other! So, because you are lukewarm—neither hot nor cold—I am about to spit you out of my mouth. [Revelation 3:15-16]*

"Lukewarm": indifferent, lacking conviction, half-hearted.

May it never be! We know that God left heaven to come to earth and redeem us through giving up his life and taking upon himself all the sins of mankind; will we dare become indifferent? Do we not want to give everything to honor and give glory to such love and sacrifice? Will we have no conviction about how we live our lives?

Send your fire, Holy Spirit, that we might live and burn with a holy conviction and burning love.

If you are going to give your heart to something or someone, give it fully, or it will become a worthless gift. It is like an adulterous spouse who vows to live in covenant, but

letter VII [laodicea]

then gives himself or herself to another, treating the vows as if they were worthless.

Who has ever gazed into the eyes of their true beloved with indifference or a half-hearted love and commitment? Surely not our beloved Bridegroom! Did the Laodicean church burn with love in the beginning? How did the flame of love burn out and become indifference? Did they become more enthralled with their reputation than their Savior?

This is profoundly sobering and causes my heart to cry out, "May it never be, Lord. Keep us from becoming lukewarm and indifferent toward our commitment and covenant that we made with you." I dare say that a person involved in New Age practices or false religion has a better chance of salvation then the one who is lukewarm and indifferent in their convictions.

"Zeal for God but not according to knowledge" (Romans 10:2) is more fertile ground for the Gospel than zeal for nothing.[2]

Even today, we are more appalled by the atheist we pass on the street than the lukewarm person sitting next to us on Sunday morning—but we should feel moved to compassion and concern, and fall to our knees, crying out for that man or woman who has settled for a form of Christianity but has denied the importance of complete surrender to the risen Christ. Such a person causes more damage to the witness of the church.

---

2   David H. Stern, *Jewish New Testament Commentary* (Clarksville, MD: Jewish New Testament Publications, Inc. 1992), 801.

VII LETTERS

The revival that we see beginning to break out will awaken many who have been stuck on fences of indifference. God will release his presence and power in a way that causes fence-dwellers to make a choice. Lukewarm churches, also, will have to decide whether to embrace revival that causes people to awaken to the fullness of God, or reject it and choose to accept compromise and dead religion. Those that compromise will discover that such foolishness leads to their demise. The churches and individuals who receive the outpouring of God's Spirit will be transformed, and they will bear the fruit that produces new wine.

> *You say, 'I am rich; I have acquired wealth and do not need a thing.' But you do not realize that you are wretched, pitiful, poor, blind and naked. I counsel you to buy from me gold refined in the fire, so you can become rich; and white clothes to wear, so you can cover your shameful nakedness; and salve to put on your eyes, so you can see. [Revelation 3:17-18]*

Isn't it interesting that the Laodicean church demonstrates how earthly wealth and privilege can be the downfall of a church that gains a great reputation and honorable name. Those of us residing in prosperous nations can relate to this scenario, because we have experienced a life of abundance compared to the rest of the world—and compared to most people throughout history! I am not saying that we will fall into the same dangerous traps, but we must be aware of our need to have the Spirit of the Lord prepare our hearts and lives. We must store up our treasures in

letter VII [laodicea]

heavenly places and place our trust in the Lord, not in the wealth of our nations.

> *The church of Laodicea...was rebuked for allowing the wealth and comfort enjoyed by the Laodiceans in general to blunt the edge of its Christian confession: materially affluent and self-sufficient, it was spiritually "wretched, pitiable, poor, blind and naked." The city's economic prosperity, eye ointment, and wool could do nothing to help this spiritual destitution.*[3]

What a tragedy and heartbreak.

The Lord desires to keep his church today from the trappings of merely having a good reputation and name. We want to honor his name by having the fruit of righteousness and purity as we stand before him. We must allow the Spirit of the Lord to help us to discern our own soul's condition. We must not get comfortable in what others think about us, but rather seek the truth of how God sees the condition of our souls. In this day of vast social media presence, almost anyone can convince the masses of the good condition of their soul. Yet, we must be sober and honest before the Lord, who knows the intent of our hearts, and the truth about the surrender of our souls to his Spirit.

We must ask the Lord to give us eyes to see into our souls so that we can allow the deep work of his Spirit to make us alive. His Spirit will search us and lead us into abundant life, free of offensive ways.

---

[3] F. F. Bruce, "Laodicea" in *The Anchor Bible Dictionary*, Volume 4 (NYC: Doubleday, 1992), 230.

VII LETTERS

Search me, God and know my heart; test me and know my anxious thoughts. See if there is any offensive way in me, and lead me in the way everlasting.
[Psalm 139:23-24]

Buy Gold

I counsel you to buy from me gold refined in the fire, so you can become rich; and white clothes to wear, so you can cover your shameful nakedness; and salve to put on your eyes, so you can see. [Revelation 3:18]

It's worth noting that the main exports of Laodicea were gold, garments, and eye salve for medicinal purposes. God knew that they would understand that they depended on the material wealth brought in by these exports, but he wanted them to import the spiritual gold, garments, and salve that bring salvation. They needed faith in God, not security in worldly wealth.

The church of Laodicea had material wealth that was worthless and useless compared to the importance of their eternal condition. Their great wealth may have been outwardly impressive, but they were impoverished before God. He counseled them to buy true wealth: gold refined in the fire. Only then would they truly be rich. The true wealth they needed was found in the wisdom Jesus gives.

The counsel of the Lord is pure gold, genuine riches that gives life to his sons and daughters. Anyone who receives the counsel of the Lord finds great riches. Wisdom is gold! And we are invited to buy this gold without money. It is given by grace.

letter VII [laodicea]

> *Come, all you who are thirsty, come to the waters; and you who have no money, come, buy and eat! Come buy wine and milk without money and without cost.*
> *[Isaiah 55:1]*

Wine is the outpouring of the Holy Spirit and milk is the Word of God. This spiritual wine and milk are the only things that will quench the thirst of our souls. Often, we seek other things to satisfy our thirst, but "drinking" from a well filled with the delights of the flesh is a counterfeit quenching. It is a temporary "fix" that creates demonic dependency, ultimately leaving us thirsting for more and never truly being filled, in an unending cycle. We eventually become malnourished and lost in despair.

The Laodiceans were also counseled to buy eye salve. This speaks of the salve of the Holy Spirit's wisdom, that gives us eyes to see with discernment. It heals the blindness that keeps us from seeing the true condition of our souls. His eye salve gives us insight into spiritual truths. The Laodicean church did not have eyes to see that they were spiritually dying. They had become blind to their filthy grave clothes.

> *Then he showed me Joshua the high priest standing before the angel of the LORD, and Satan standing at his right side to accuse him. The LORD said to Satan, "The LORD rebuke you, Satan! The LORD, who has chosen Jerusalem, rebuke you! Is not this man a burning stick snatched from the fire?"*
> *Now Joshua was dressed in filthy clothes as he stood before the angel. The angel said to those who were*

VII LETTERS

> *standing before him, "Take off his filthy clothes."*
> *Then he said to Joshua, "See, I have taken away your*
> *sin, and I will put fine garments on you."*
> *Then I said, "Put a clean turban on his head." So they*
> *put a clean turban on his head and clothed him, while*
> *the angel of the LORD stood by.*
> *The angel of the LORD gave this charge to Joshua:*
> *"This is what the LORD Almighty says: 'If you will walk*
> *in obedience to me and keep my requirements, then*
> *you will govern my house and have charge of my courts,*
> *and I will give you a place among these standing here.*
> *[Zechariah 3:1-7]*

In the same way, the Laodicean church needed a miraculous resurrection and their graveclothes removed. Likewise, many believers in our day are in need of miraculous intervention as we walk through this season that seems to be rapidly approaching the final hours of human history.

We must ask God for the true gold of his Word and his counsel, eye salve from the Holy Spirit that opens our hearts to see our true condition, and clean garments free from the pollution of this world. Satan has held many sons and daughters captive to deception and bondage. He entices them with false security and pride in material wealth; he pollutes their eyes with impurities until they are blind to spiritual truth, not aware of their wretched condition. They can't see that they are naked and filthy.

As the outpouring of the Holy Spirit comes, people will suddenly receive insight to their true spiritual condition and repentance will fall upon them. Like the father in

letter VII [laodicea]

the parable of the prodigal son, God will rush to them and clothe them with clean robes. He will place rings upon their fingers and he will celebrate with great joy and feasting. We will see God snatch many from the fire of hell's eternal grip.

A great number of our sons and daughters have been deceived and defiled, and the Spirit of the Lord is allowing us to stand with him and say, "The Lord rebuke you, Satan!" The Lord will save our sons and daughters! He will snatch them from the fire of eternal separation from God. He will clothe them in clean garments and restore them to right standing with him.

> *Those whom I love I rebuke and discipline. So be earnest and repent. Here I am! I stand at the door and knock. If anyone hears my voice and opens the door, I will come in and eat with that person, and they with me.*
> [Revelation 3:19-20]

Often readers view this seventh letter as a harsh rebuke; but I believe it is not harsh—it is passionate!. It is one of the greatest love letters ever written because it comes from the intense agape love of God, who desires that none perish, but all come to repentance. His love for the Laodicean church is clearly displayed, as well as his deep grief that they have lost their way and do not know it. Jesus was jealous for their affections and their restoration to him. He called for them to return to him quickly and sincerely in true repentance.

The everlasting God stood at the door of their hearts and knocked. He longed for them to open to him once

VII LETTERS

again, to hear his voice and be restored as sons and daughters. He held in his hand all that they needed to be spiritually nourished so they would truly flourish with spiritual riches.

It is the same in our day. No matter how far we have fallen, he draws near and calls to us to open our hearts and let him return. He longs for us to be united with him in oneness and to receive the eternal inheritance he died to give us. He is the Lover of our souls, and as a Good Shepherd, he will use his rod to correct our course back to the safety of his love and ways. His pursuit of us is an unimaginable act of pure love.

I first heard of salvation through Jesus when I was a fourteen-year-old teen. I foolishly and blindly remained in my sin, fearful of what I might lose. The Lord stood at the door of my heart for four years, knocking continuously, whispering tenderly of his love, until I came to my senses and received him as my Lord and Savior when I was eighteen. When I opened the door to him, what a feast he had prepared for me to partake with him! I did not know that what I had so fiercely clung to was a cheap substitute for true love.

Ever since that day, I have been feasting upon the rich bounty of his love and goodness.

> *To the one who is victorious, I will give the right to sit with me on my throne, just as I was victorious and sat down with my Father on his throne. Whoever has ears, let them hear what the Spirit says to the churches.*
> [Revelation 3:21-22]

letter VII [laodicea]

This letter's conclusion speaks of God's great hope regarding the Laodicean church. He prays for them to overcome their bondage. He gives them a promise if only they will repent.

Jesus overcame all temptation, and he now sits on a throne next to his Father. He promises that those who overcome will enter his victory and sit with him in oneness as his bride. He invites them to buy spiritual riches so they will receive his promise. If they repent and turn, they will be forgiven and victorious. What a beautiful and powerful promise.

In his mercy, the Lord extends his promise to generations yet to come. If we enter his victory, we will be given the right to sit with him on his throne. Matthew Henry wrote a beautiful description:

That those who are conformed to Christ in his trials and victories shall be conformed to him in his glory; they shall sit down with him on his throne, on his throne of judgment at the end of the world, on his throne of glory to all eternity, shining in his beams by virtue of their union with him and relation to him, as the mystical body of which he is the head.

We will be eternally rich in love, oneness, unity, and glory as we overcome trials and take part in his victory. This is our "Amen." It is his ultimate promise, eternally glorious and worthy of any trials we must overcome.

Afterword

Most of this book was written as I sat before the Lord in 2021 and 2022. As I wrote in the introduction, at that time I kept sensing the Lord telling his people "Take heed!" I heard then—and hear even to this day—an "echo" of old resonating through the millennia, the sound that arises from the faith of believers through the ages.

In my spirit, I hear the sound of the faith responses from men like Noah, Abraham, and Moses, as well as men and women not mentioned in the Old Testament. I also hear the sound of those who first believed in Jesus when he walked the earth. And I hear these sounds intermingling with the sound of thousands upon thousands of believers in Yeshua who have continued to follow him. It is the sound of faith—the release of prayer, praise, obedience, and surrender—converging with the sound believers are releasing to this day, in this hour, and it is like the sound of many waters roaring as one (Revelation 14:2).

In late June, 2024, I became aware that this "sound" would break a *sound barrier*. I didn't understand what that meant, so I asked the Lord.

He said: *"The sound will break the barrier of deception."*

Deception has written a narrative on the hearts and within the minds of those who walk the earth today—a counterfeit in direct opposition to the Lord's promised new covenant:

> "...I will put my law in their minds
> and write it on their hearts.
> I will be their God,
> and they will be my people" [Jeremiah 31:33]

This vile deception seeks to kill, steal, and destroy our children and our children's children—our future. It seeks to silence the sound of truth, faith, hope, and love that only comes from surrendering our lives to Jesus and following his ways. The sound of deception has infiltrated every mountain of influence: religion, family, government, education, media, arts/entertainment, and business.

But there is a pure sound. It is a sound of the generations of those who walked by faith and lived in truth. It is the sound of those who responded to the counsel of Yeshua, who loves us, and who disciplines those he loves [Revelation 3:19]. It is the sound of the faithful who stood against the darkness and followed God even into impossible situations. It is the sound of footsteps that brought the gospel of truth to the sick and the poor. It is the sound of surrender, the sound of every "yes" given in obedience to his voice, the sound of songs of praise, and the sound of groanings too deep for words. It is the sound of the Bride. It is the sound of those who respond to the ancient wisdom we have been discussing in the seven letters.

It is the sound of overcomers.

There is a convergence of the pure sound of those who lived by faith in the past combining with our release of faith today, becoming one sound.

The Lord told me, "*This is not an old sound but a **now sound**. I live outside of time, and this sound exists outside of time.*"

I came to understand that Abraham's "yes" to obeying the Lord is just as valid today as if he had just said it yesterday. Abraham's "yes" joins in heaven with our "yes" today. This is true for every man, woman, or child who has ever chosen to follow the Lord. Our trust and prayers have not been unnoticed or forgotten [Exodus 3:7; Psalm 56:8; Isaiah 65:24; Malachi 3:16; Luke 18:6-8; Acts 10:4; Revelation 5:8, 8:3-4].

Faith has a sound! It sets ears free to hear truth again. This pure sound will break the lies of deception that so many have listened to, robbing them of the knowledge of truth, God's identity, and the path to salvation.

We have examined how the enemy sought to silence the sound of God's faithful in the early church by warring against them with targeted attacks and deception. Yet, even amid the onslaught, Yeshua called to his people to HEAR his voice of truth and respond.

We too must rise up as never before to give our "yes" to the Lord. We must not allow our faith to lose its sound. We must not be silent. Your sound, your song, your surrender are the weapons that will shatter the sound of deception and release the Breaker.

> *The Breaker [the Messiah, who opens the way] shall go up before them [liberating them]. They will break out, pass through the gate and go out; so their King goes on before them, the Lord at their head*
> *[Micah 2:13, AMPCE].*

We live in a *kairos*[1] time when our Breaker is opening the way of revival for his people and allowing us to give birth to long-awaited promises. The rushing waters of the songs of generations will revive what we may have been tempted to think was lost forever. Let faith arise, and let the sound of trust and hope break the sound of deception.

This is our time to respond to the ancient invitation:

> *"Whoever has ears, let him hear what the Spirit says to the churches."*

---

[1] A Greek word meaning "time or season"; used to represent a fitting season or opportunity.

Sources

Blaiklock, E. M. "Nicolaitans" in *The New Bible Dictionary* Edited by J. D. Douglas. Grand Rapids, MI: Wm. B. Eerdmans, 1979.

Bruce, F. F. "Laodicea" in *The Anchor Bible Dictionary, Volume 4*. Edited by David Noel Freedman. New York: Doubleday, 1992.

———. "Revelation" in *The International Bible Commentary*. Edited by F. F. Bruce. Grand Rapids, MI: Zondervan, 1986.

Collins, Adela Yarbro. "Revelation, Book of" in *The Anchor Bible Dictionary, Volume 5*. Edited by David Noel Freedman. New York: Doubleday, 1992.

Dictionary of Biblical Imagery. "Revelation, Book of." Edited by Leland Ryken, James C. Wilhoit, and Tremper Longman III. Downers Grove, IL: InterVarsity Press, 1998.

Henry, Matthew. "Revelation" in *Commentary on the Whole Bible*. Posted on Bible Study Tools. https://www.biblestudytools.com/commentaries/matthew-henry-complete/revelation/

Intrator, Keith (Asher) & Juster, Dan. *Israel, the Church, and the Last Days*. Shippensburg, PA: Destiny Image, 2003.

Juster, Daniel C. ThD. *Passover, the Key that Unlocks the Book of Revelation*. Clarksville, MD: Lederer Books, 2011.

Kennedy, Titus. *The Essential Archaeological Guide to Bible Lands*. Eugene, OR: Harvest House, 2023.

Ngundu, Onesimus. "Revelation" in *Africa Bible Commentary*. Edited by Dr. Tokunboh Adeyemo. Grand Rapids, MI: Zondervan, 2006.

Stern, David H. *Jewish New Testament Commentary*. Clarksville, MD: Jewish New Testament Publications, Inc., 1992.

About the Author

Kathi Pelton is a wife, mother, and grandmother as well as an author and prophetic voice to the church. She and her husband Jeffrey pray to see God's original intent fulfilled on the earth, and together have spent years helping people encounter the healing love and mercy of God. Their passion is to see the establishment of genuine family gathered in the unity expressed in John 17.

Kathi and Jeffrey married in 1983 and together raised four children. They currently have five grandchildren, and are filled with eager expectations of many more!

The Peltons live in the Portland, Oregon region and attend Father's House Church, where they serve as part of the leadership team.

www.ingramcontent.com/pod-product-compliance
Lightning Source LLC
Chambersburg PA
CBHW060531080526
44586CB00012B/697